From Your Friends At **The MAILBOX**®

NOVEMBER

A MONTH OF IDEAS AT YOUR FINGERTIPS!

GRADES 1–3

WRITTEN BY

Shari Abbey, Sherri Beckwith, Pam Kucks,
Kerry Ireland-Miller, Nancy Matthews, Trish Pecuch,
Stacie Stone, Carmel F. White, Kathy Wolf

EDITED BY

Lynn Bemer Coble, Jennifer Rudisill, Gina Sutphin, Kathy Wolf

ILLUSTRATED BY

Jennifer Tipton Bennett, Cathy Spangler Bruce,
Teresa Davidson, Clevell Harris, Sheila Krill,
Becky J. Radtke, Rebecca Saunders,
Donna K. Teal

TYPESET BY

Lynette Maxwell

COVER DESIGNED BY

Jennifer Tipton Bennett

www.themailbox.com

©1996 by THE EDUCATION CENTER, INC.
All rights reserved.
ISBN #1-56234-123-5

Manufactured in the United States
10 9 8 7 6 5 4

TABLE OF CONTENTS

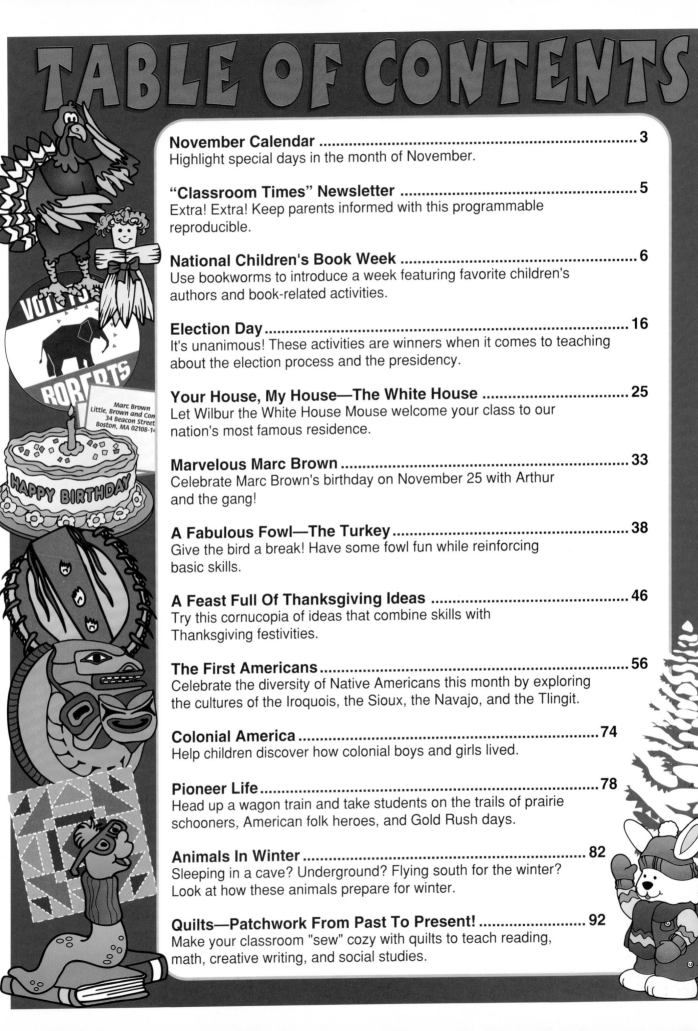

November Calendar

International Drum Month

Plan to celebrate International Drum Month sometime during November. Share the book *Max Found Two Sticks* by Brian Pinkney (Simon & Schuster Trade, 1994). Then have band members from your local high school visit the classroom to show students some different types of drums such as bass or snare drums. Invite the band members to play their drums for students. Have students compare the sounds and repeat rhythms.

Peanut Butter Lovers' Month

Crunch into some nutty fun when you celebrate Peanut Butter Lovers' Month! Read the book *From Peanuts To Peanut Butter* by Melvin Berger (Newbridge Communications, Inc.; 1992). Afterward make peanut butter with the help of your students. To make peanut butter you'll need 2 cups of fresh-roasted peanuts (shelled), 4 tablespoons of vegetable oil, 4 teaspoons of sugar, 1 teaspoon of salt, and a blender. Put all of the ingredients into a blender and mix them until smooth. Let each student sample a bit of the peanut butter after spreading it on a cracker. Or use the peanut butter with the Sandwich Day activity (see November 3).

1—National Authors' Day

Annually held on November 1, National Authors' Day is a day set aside to show appreciation for the people who have written American literature. Plan to hold an Authors' Day celebration in your classroom on this day. Invite a local author to visit your classroom to read some of her works. Or allow each child to share a story written by his favorite author. Spotlight student authors by allowing them to share their favorite works. Conclude the event by having an Authors' Tea—complete with cookies, juice, and tea.

3—Sandwich Day

This day is held in conjunction with the birth anniversary of John Montague, Fourth Earl Of Sandwich, who was born on this date in 1718. While playing cards, Montague ordered a servant to bring him a piece of meat between two slices of bread. This enabled him to eat and play cards at the same time. Read the book *Make Me A Peanut Butter Sandwich And A Glass Of Milk* by Ken Robbins (Scholastic Inc., 1992) or *Peanut Butter And Jelly: A Play Rhyme* by Nadine Bernard Westcott (Dutton Children's Books, 1987). Then let each student make a peanut butter sandwich using two slices of bread, some peanut butter (see Peanut Butter Lovers' Month), and a plastic knife. After each student has made and eaten his sandwich, challenge him to list the steps involved in making a peanut butter sandwich.

9—Birth Date Of Lois Ehlert

Celebrate Lois Ehlert's birthday by sharing *Red Leaf, Yellow Leaf* (Scholastic Inc., 1991)—one of the many books that this prolific author has written. Once students have seen the striking collage illustrations in Ehlert's books, no doubt they'll be anxious to give this marvelous medium a whirl. Provide students with a variety of materials—such as newspaper, wallpaper samples, felt, construction paper, tissue paper, and fabric scraps—so they can make their own collages.

11—Veterans Day

Prior to Veterans Day, invite a local veteran to visit your classroom to talk about his or her experiences while in the armed services. Explain to students that Veterans Day honors those men and women who have served in the armed services for the United States. Tell students that Veterans Day celebrations often include parades and speeches. Special services are also held at the Tomb of the Unknown Soldier in Arlington National Cemetery.

14—Birth Date Of William Steig

Honor this author on his birthday by reading *Sylvester And The Magic Pebble* (Silver Burdett Press, 1992). Ask each student to draw a picture showing what she would wish for if she had a magic pebble. Encourage each student to write a story to accompany her picture. Then give each child a small "magic" pebble.

15—Birth Date Of Georgia O'Keeffe

Born on this date in 1887 in Wisconsin, Georgia O'Keeffe is known for her paintings of nature and her landscapes of the American Southwest. Use the book *Georgia O'Keeffe: Painter Of The Desert* by Jacqueline Ball and Catherine Conant (Blackbirch Press™, 1991) or *Georgia O'Keeffe* by Robyn M. Turner (Little, Brown & Co.; 1991) to show your students some of this artist's works. Then have each student use tempera paints and paintbrushes to paint a desert scene on a sheet of construction paper. Challenge older students by having them research plants and animals to include in the scene.

American Education Week (Annually, the week preceding the week with Thanksgiving)

The goal of American Education Week is to spotlight the importance of public education. Plan to hold an Open House in your classroom sometime during American Education Week. Invite parents to visit your classroom to see the accomplishments of their children. Have samples of your students' work displayed in the classroom for parents to see.

19—The Anniversary Of The Gettysburg Address

Tell students that the Gettysburg Address was delivered by Abraham Lincoln on this date in 1863. Although the speech was less than two minutes long, it is considered one of the best speeches in American history. Share Jean Fritz's book *Just A Few Words, Mr. Lincoln: The Story of The Gettysburg Address* (Grosset & Dunlap, Inc.; 1993) to help students understand more about this important speech.

Great American Smokeout (Annually, the third Thursday in November)

Explain to students that the Great American Smokeout is a day set aside to help smokers kick the habit. Discuss with students the disadvantages and health risks associated with smoking; then have each student make a poster encouraging people to quit smoking—or to not even start smoking. Gain permission from area doctors, dentists, and business people to hang the posters in their buildings.

CLASSROOM TIMES

Teacher:_____ Date:_____

NOVEMBER

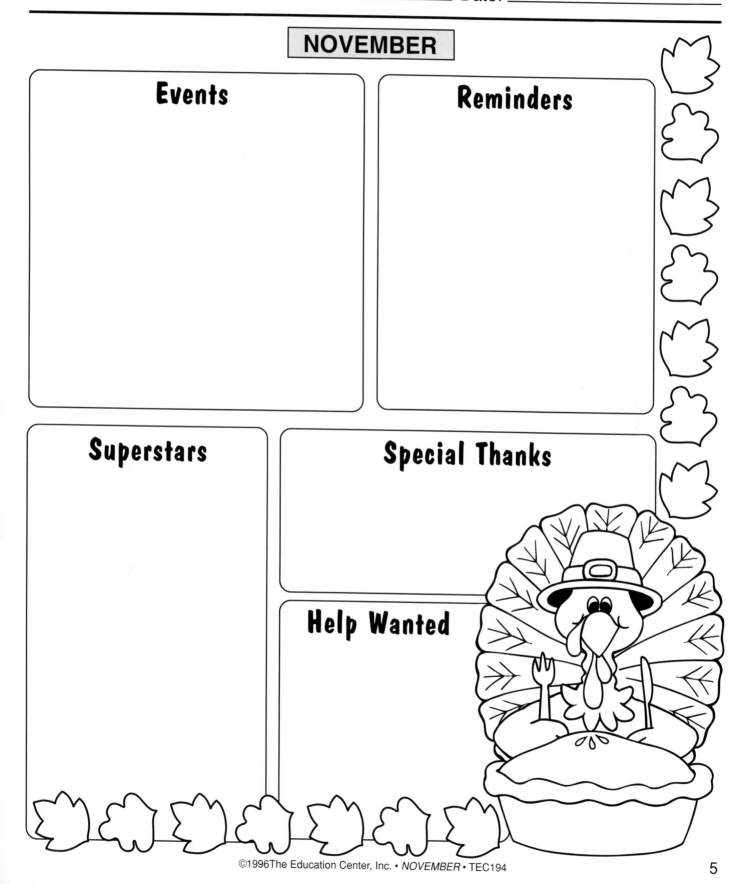

Events

Reminders

Superstars

Special Thanks

Help Wanted

NATIONAL CHILDREN'S BOOK WEEK

Worm your way into reading with this collection of activities to celebrate National Children's Book Week.

ideas by Shari Abbey and Kathy Wolf

BOOKWORM BOOKMARKS

Begin a week of celebrating children's books by supplying your students with the necessary tools—bookmarks! Duplicate the bookmark and bookworm patterns from page 11 on white construction paper for each student. Have each student cut out the bookmark along the solid line and fold along the dotted line so that it makes a small book. Next have her cut out and color her bookworm and add two wiggle eyes. After the student has decorated the front cover of her bookmark, have her glue the bookworm to the inside so that it peeks over the top. Each time the student finishes a book, she writes the title on the back of the bookmark and colors in a bookworm. Present the "Bona Fide Bookworm" award on page 11 to those readers who color in all five worms. These bookmarks are sure to wiggle their way into children's books!

Get between the covers

of a good book!

National Children's Book Week November ___ 1996

TAKE A BITE OUT OF READING!

Encourage students to read some deliciously good books with this wonderfully wormy reading-incentive program. Create a bulletin board of bookworms to motivate students to take a bite out of reading each day. Cover your bulletin board with yellow background paper. Duplicate the leaf pattern on page 13 on green construction paper for each child to cut out. Duplicate the worm patterns on page 11 on different colors of construction paper. Give one worm to each student to cut out and label with his name. Supply each student with a pair of wiggle eyes to glue to his worm cutout. Have students glue the worms to their leaf cutouts. Pin the worms on the board as shown. Each time a student finishes reading a book, he punches a hole at the edge of his leaf with a hole puncher. Students will love watching their progress as their leaves disappear. How many good books can your little bookworms devour?

TAKE A BITE OUT OF READING!

GRAND ENTRANCES

Get students involved in a schoolwide celebration of books with a grand entrance for every classroom. Prior to National Children's Book Week, ask each of your colleagues to select an author to promote with a display on her classroom door. Provide the sign-up sheet on page 14 or ask your librarian to create a sign-up list of best-known children's authors to ensure that each class will feature a different author and title.

Enlist the help of your class in selecting a favorite book from the list. Read the book aloud and ask students how they would convince others to read the book using an eye-catching door display. Divide your class into groups and have each group help with the design of the grand entrance on or around the door. During Book Week allow students to take a book walk through the halls and vote on the best grand entrances. Award books donated by local stores to the winning classes.

BOOK BARTERING

Here's a sure way to get your students to browse their bookshelves. Hold a used paperback book exchange in your classroom. Several days ahead of the exchange, inform parents of your plan and invite students to bring in at least one paperback book from home. Give each student a ticket (page 13) for each book he brings. On the day of the exchange, display all the books in a special area and allow students to browse the titles. Students may exchange their tickets for "new" used books. You may want to have a Book Barter Day every month!

ADOPT-A-BOOK PROJECT

Oh, those poor, unattractive books that sit on the library shelves all year. No one ever checks them out because of their dusty, lackluster appearance. Help your students remember the saying, "You can't judge a book by its cover" with this spiffy idea. Ask your librarian for help in choosing several of those seldom-checked-out books that would be suitable for your grade level. Give each student a book to adopt. Have the student read the book and then design a new book jacket. In addition to a beautiful new front cover, have the student include author and illustrator information and a summary of the book on the inside flaps. Then, with your librarian's help, display the new and improved books in a special area of the library. Those adopted books will be checked out again in no time.

Horton Hatches The Egg

Green Eggs And Ham

One Fish Two Fish Red Fish Blue Fish

Fox In Socks

The Cat In The Hat

READ A BOOK BY DR. SEUSS!

Hunches In Bunches

Hop On Pop

BOOK WEEK BOOK TOUR

Explain to students that publishers often send authors on book tours to promote their titles and sell more books. You may indeed entice an author to visit your school for a book talk by contacting the publisher. If this is not possible, your students can still simulate a book campaign to generate support for reading.

Divide your class into pairs and have each pair decide on a favorite book to promote. Give each pair the choice of promoting its book by writing an ad, drawing a poster, creating a song, dressing up as characters from the story, or making the book into a movie. Older students can also do research to report about the author and illustrator and then display other titles by the same author. Arrange for your students to visit other classrooms or the library to present their books on tour. As the students embrace their favorite authors, they will encourage others to read them, too!

The Magic School Bus

1. big
2. hairy
3. red
4. lovable
5. friendly

WHO ARE THESE CHARACTERS?

Celebrate your favorite books in a big way. Brainstorm a list of your students' favorite fictional characters such as Ms. Frizzle, Amelia Bedelia, Clifford, etc. Then pair students to create larger-than-life book characters. Have each pair choose one character to illustrate. Tell students that their characters should be two to three feet tall. Supply each pair with a large sheet of bulletin-board paper, various colors of construction paper, and markers. Next give each pair one 8 1/2" x 11" sheet of construction paper to fold in half like a card. Ask each pair to list five adjectives that describe its character on the outside of the card and write the character's name on the inside. Display each character in the hallway with the descriptive card beside it. Add the title "Who Are These Characters?" As they walk past these fictional folks, teachers, students, and visitors will enjoy trying to guess the characters.

GET PUBLISHED!

Motivate your would-be authors to write about their favorite books. Duplicate the book-review form on page 12 for each child to complete. Share samples of book reviews published in newspapers or book catalogs; then help students choose books to write about. Practice filling out a book-review form together; then allow students to complete their copies. Submit the student reviews to your local newspaper for publication. With some notice, most small newspapers will gladly publish student-written material. Some papers may even have limited space for artwork. To spur community awareness, write up an introduction for the submission stating that this project was done to celebrate National Children's Book Week.

A PARADE OF CHARACTERS

What's a celebration without a parade? Take your celebration of National Children's Book Week schoolwide with this showstopping idea. Several weeks in advance, send a note home to parents explaining that children are going to dress up as book characters on a specified date. Plenty of notice will be appreciated by parents in order for them to help their children decide upon characters and create costumes. A week or two before your scheduled parade, have each student announce the character he is going to portray and write three to four sentences telling about his character—including whom he is, what story he is in and what he does in the story, the author who created him, and books in which others could read more about him. Older students may be encouraged to memorize these lines. Be sure to allow time for students to practice. Direct your youngsters to say their lines loudly and clearly. Arrange to visit other classrooms with your parade of characters during National Children's Book Week.

On the day of the parade, have several volunteers on hand to help students get into their costumes. Line children up in single file, and march from room to room so students can show off their costumes and say their lines. This is one parade that is sure to get rave reviews!

LITERARY LUNCHEON

End the last chapter of your celebration of books with a surprise twist in the plot. Ask your students to bring a sack lunch on the last day of National Children's Book Week. With approval from your librarian, take your students to the library to eat lunch among the literature. If possible, invite a storyteller, local celebrity, or community leader as a guest reader to provide entertainment while your kids munch on their lunches.

FOR BOOKWORMS ONLY

Turn your wiggle worms into bookworms with these books about books.

FROM PICTURES TO WORDS: A BOOK ABOUT MAKING A BOOK

by Janet Stevens
(Holiday House, Inc.; 1995)
Janet Stevens is an illustrator until her characters talk her into becoming a writer too. She and her lovable characters take readers step-by-step through the process of writing a story for publishing. Share this story with your young writers, taking time to discuss the terminology such as *character, plot, setting,* and *problem.* Duplicate the reproducible on page 15 and let your students put Janet Stevens's method into practice. Once the reproducible is completed, have each student follow the outline he created to write his story. All that's left is the publishing! Each student may want to make a construction-paper cover for his story individually, or you can bind all the stories into a class anthology.

MORE BOOKS ABOUT BOOKS

The Library
by Sarah Stewart
(Farrar, Straus & Giroux, Inc.;1995)

Sophie And Sammy's Library Sleepover
by Judith Caseley
(Greenwillow Books, 1993)

Fix-it
by David McPhail
(E. P. Dutton, 1984)

I Took My Frog To The Library
by Eric A. Kimmel
(Viking, 1990)

My Hometown Library
by William Jaspersohn
(Houghton Mifflin Company, 1994)

THE YOUNG AUTHOR'S DO-IT-YOURSELF BOOK: HOW TO WRITE, ILLUSTRATE, AND PRODUCE YOUR OWN BOOK

by Donna Guthrie, Nancy Bentley, and Katy Keck Arnsteen
(The Millbrook Press, 1994)
Get ready to start rolling books off the presses after sharing this informative, entertaining book with your students. Students will enjoy the tour through the writing process: from just getting an idea, to developing a plot, and finally to promoting a book, with much more information in between. Armed with motivation and information, your students are likely to put on their authors' hats before you even finish the book.

A day before sharing this book, ask each student to bring a hat from home. For each student, write the word "Author" on a 3" x 5" index card. After sharing the story, have each student tape the index card on the front of her hat and put the hat on. Inform your students that they now have their "authors' hats" on. You may want to reread the section on "Writing." Then let the ideas start flowing.

Encourage your authors to follow the steps listed in the book: from author, to editor, to illustrator, to binder, to promotion. When a student is ready to advance to the next step, have her change hats (by putting a new label on her hat, such as "Editor"). Have students wear their hats each day during writing time so that you can see at a glance where each student is in the writing process. Use an idea from the book, such as throwing an author party, to promote the books when they are finished.

Get between the covers

of a good book!

National Children's Book Week

November

_____

Books I've read this week:

_____   _____

_____   _____

_____   _____

Bookworm Pattern
Use with "Bookworm Bookmarks" and "Take A Bite Out Of Reading!" on page 6.

Award
Use with "Bookworm Bookmarks" on page 6.

Name _____

Is A Bona Fide Bookworm!

Signed _____

A KID'S REVIEW OF A KID'S BOOK

Book Reviewer: _____ Age: _____

Title: _____

Author: _____

Illustrator: _____

Publisher: _____

Copyright Date: _____

I give this book ☆ ☆ ☆ : _____

because: _____

_____

_____

_____

_____

_____

Note To The Teacher: Use with "Get Published!" on page 8.

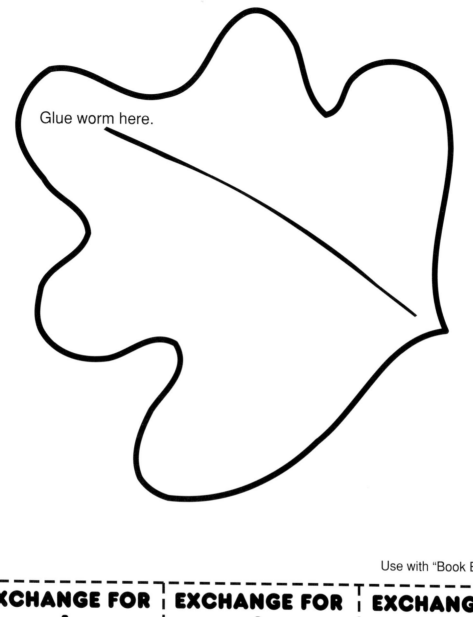

Glue worm here.

EXCHANGE FOR 1 NEW USED BOOK!

EXCHANGE FOR 1 NEW USED BOOK!

EXCHANGE FOR 1 NEW USED BOOK!

EXCHANGE FOR 1 NEW USED BOOK!

EXCHANGE FOR 1 NEW USED BOOK!

EXCHANGE FOR 1 NEW USED BOOK!

CHOOSE A FAVORITE CHILDREN'S BOOK AUTHOR!

Aardema, Verna
Adler, David A.
Ahlberg, Janet and Allan
Aliki
Allard, Harry
Andersen, Hans Christian
Arnold, Tedd
Barrett, Judi
Bemelmans, Ludwig
Berenstain, Stan and Jan
Bianco, Margery Williams
Blume, Judy
Brett, Jan
Bridwell, Norman
Brown, Marc
Byars, Betsy
Carle, Eric
Catling, Patrick S.
Caudill, Rebecca
Cleary, Beverly
Cohen, Miriam
Cole, Joanna
Crews, Donald
Danziger, Paula
dePaola, Tomie
Dr. Seuss
Eastman, P. D.
Freeman, Don
Gibbons, Gail
Giff, Patricia Reilly
Goble, Paul
Henkes, Kevin
Hoban, Lillian and Russell
Howe, James

Hurwitz, Johanna
Keats, Ezra Jack
Kellogg, Steven
Kline, Suzy
Lionni, Leo
Lobel, Arnold
MacLachlan, Patricia
Marshall, James
Martin Jr., Bill
Mayer, Mercer
McCloskey, Robert
McKissack, Patricia C.
Minarik, Else Holmelund
Noble, Trinka Hakes
Numeroff, Laura Joffee
Parish, Peggy
Peet, Bill
Polacco, Patricia
Rey, H. A. and Margret
Rylant, Cynthia
Sendak, Maurice
Sharmat, Marjorie Weinman
Silverstein, Shel
Steig, William
Stevenson, James
Van Allsburg, Chris
Viorst, Judith
Warner, Gertrude Chandler
Wells, Rosemary
White, E. B.
Wilder, Laura Ingalls
Wood, Don and Audrey
Yolen, Jane
Zolotow, Charlotte

Put your classroom on the Book Tour. Circle your favorite author to promote during National Children's Book Week!

Teacher _____

Grade _____

Note To The Teacher: Use with "Grand Entrances" on page 7.

BUILD A STORY

1. Who are your *characters*? Draw and name them.
   Use the back if you need more room.

_____ _____ _____

2. What will the *setting* be? _____

3. What is the *plot?* (What will the characters do?) _____

_____

_____

4. What *problem* do the characters run into? _____

_____

5. Think of two ways the characters try to solve the problem.
   A. _____
   B. _____

6. Finally the characters find a solution that works. What is it? _____

_____

_____

7. How does your story end? _____

_____

_____

Note To The Teacher: *Use with From Pictures To Words: A Book About Making A Book* on page 10.

Election Day

Although your class discussions about choosing the next president will start early in the school year, designate the week before Election Day as Election Week in your classroom. Elect this unit to teach students about the election process and the presidency.

ideas by Pam Kucks, Trish Pecuch, and Kathy Wolf

If I Were President...

Ask students what they know about the current president. Discuss questions like "Is he up for reelection? What has he accomplished while in office?" Write students' thoughts on a chart; then share this list of some presidential duties:

- Meets with world leaders
- Nominates U.S. officials (cabinet members, Supreme Court justices); appoints ambassadors to other countries
- Recommends new laws for Congress to pass
- Follows the Constitution to make sure all federal laws are enforced
- Protects the rights of the people
- Prepares the national budget
- Issues executive orders such as proclamations
- Serves as commander in chief of the armed forces
- Leads his political party
- Attends ceremonies, dinners, and other events as chief of state

Share the book *If I Were President* compiled by Peggy Gavan (Troll Associates, 1994) with your class. Students will enjoy hearing how other children answered the question, "What would *you* do if you were elected President of the United States?" Ask each student to write a paragraph telling what he would do if he were president. Mount the students' papers on red or blue construction paper. Bind the students' writings into a class book with the title "If I Were President...."

Who Has Presidential Potential?

Tell students that the office of president of the United States is filled every four years by a national election. The president must be a natural-born citizen, be at least 35 years old, and have lived in the United States for 14 years. If a president is running for his second four-year term in office, he is called the *incumbent* president. For critical thinking, ask students to list eight to ten qualities that make someone a good president. Take a vote to find out which quality your students think is most important. Then ask students to tell which candidate they think would make the best leader and why.

Read *The Election Book: People Pick A President* by Tamara Hanneman (Scholastic Inc., 1992) for details about the presidents, elections, primaries, and conventions.

"We're Proud To Be Americans!"

Read the book *Voting And Elections* by Dennis B. Fradin (Childrens Press™, 1985) to your class and discuss the election process with students. Then have students brainstorm a list of presidential- and election-related vocabulary words to create a patriotic bulletin board. Write each vocabulary word on a star cutout. Enlarge, color, and cut out the characters on page 23. Cover your bulletin board with white background paper and mount the characters as shown. Have students help you create a border by pinning the stars in ABC order. Add the title "We're Proud To Be Americans!" Refer to this board for spelling and creative writing throughout this unit. Reproduce the word search on page 22 to reinforce election-related vocabulary.

A Voter Registration Drive

Preparing for a classroom election is a good way to help students understand how elections work. Tell students that although voting is a right, voters must meet certain requirements to vote. A voter must be 18 years of age or older, a citizen of the USA, and registered. A voter can only vote at the polling place in the *precinct* where he or she lives.

Since registration is an important step in being able to vote, you'll want to conduct a voter registration drive in your classroom before Election Week. Provide a copy of the form on page 21 for each student. Help students complete the forms, and keep them on file for use at your class polling place.

17

Campaign Power

Explain to your class that every campaign has its own slogans and ads. Campaign committees look for creative ways to convince people to vote for their candidates. Candidates try to reach as many voters as possible with their messages of "Vote For Me!" by paying for TV commercials, newspaper ads, posters, and billboards. Campaign workers ask people to display yard signs or wear buttons to show support for their candidates.

Divide your class into campaign teams for some creative thinking. Contact local political-party headquarters to obtain sample buttons, posters, signs, and banners if possible. Or ask parents if they have campaign memorabilia that they would be willing to put on display in your classroom. Then have your students work in pairs to create a campaign poster, hat, banner, button, or song for the candidate of their choice. Display the results in the hallway for some schoolwide voter reaction!

"Let's Take A Vote!"

Explain that "an unofficial vote to show the relative support for the different candidates" is called a *straw vote* or a *straw poll*. Take a straw poll in your class to find out who is favored to win the presidential race. List the presidential candidates' names on a bar graph as shown. Let each student add a star sticker to the graph to indicate his or her choice for president. Save these results and compare them to the results from your classroom mock election and the real presidential election. Did your students correctly predict the next president?

Stand Up And Be Counted!

Explain to your class that there are many ways of voting. These include *a show of hands, a voice vote, a roll call vote, an absentee ballot,* and *a secret ballot.* Discuss how each kind of vote is taken. Ask students why it is important to have private or confidential voting as well as fair and accurate counting.

Then have students make ballot boxes and cast their ballots on student-generated issues. To prepare for Voting Day, have each student decide what he wants his classmates to vote on, such as changes in the school lunch menu, new class rules, or favorite sports teams. Give each student the homework assignment of decorating a shoebox to look like a ballot box. Once the ballot boxes arrive at school, have each student write out and post his proposition, giving two choices for the voters. Duplicate a large supply of the official ballot on page 21 and a class roster to place beside each ballot box.

On Voting Day, remind students of the importance of secret balloting and the right to their own opinions. Have each student place his shoebox on his desk and hand out ballots as classmates arrive at his polling place. To make sure each student votes only once on each issue, election officials check off voters' names on a class roster. After a designated time, have each student empty his shoebox and count the votes under the watchful eye of another student. Once the votes have been tallied, let students share their results. These ballot boxes are a shoo-in when it comes to election fun!

Campaign Buttons

Get into the spirit of the presidential election by having students make campaign buttons to wear or display on their desks. Duplicate the patterns on page 24 on colored construction paper for each child to cut out. Write the names of the presidential candidates on the board. Have the student fill in her candidate's name and stick on gold stars as shown. Laminate the buttons if desired. With a hot-glue gun, attach red or blue ribbons and a safety pin to the back of each button. Allow students to wear their buttons the week preceding Election Day.

To extend this idea, your class can show their patriotic spirit by making buttons and presenting them to voters as they leave the polls. Check with local election officials well in advance to see if student volunteers—with adult supervision—can stand at community polling places and pass out "I Have Voted!" buttons.

Voting Booth Bonus

To prepare for a mock election, make a cardboard voting booth from a large appliance box. Cut off the top and leave the front open. Hang a curtain across the front. Have your students decorate an official ballot box and place it inside the booth on a desk or table. Program one copy of the official ballot on page 21 and duplicate enough for your class. Appoint election officials to check off registered voters on your class roster, provide ballots, empty the ballot box, and tally the votes. If your school is an actual polling place, your students may be able to see the voting process firsthand. (Check with election officials in advance.) Then return to the classroom and have students cast their ballots.

As the ballots are counted, record the votes on a wall chart or graph. If other classes are holding mock elections too, exchange results. When all "precincts" are in, add the results for a school total. On the next day, engage in some election analysis. Did your school vote reflect the national or state results?

To build grassroots support for classroom democracy, keep your voting booth set up all year long. Plan to vote on one meaningful class issue each week. Important issues might include the next book to read aloud to the class, the best night for homework assignments, or the best reward for good work. Students will enjoy voting for something new and real each week.

Use the registration form with "A Voter Registration Drive" on page 17.

Classroom Voter Registration Form

1 Name		2 Age
3 Address		
4 Date Of Birth	5 Birthplace	
6 Grade	7 Teacher	

Use the ballot with "Stand Up And Be Counted" on page 19.

Cast Your Ballot!

☐ _____

☐ _____

★★★★★★★

Election Day Challenge

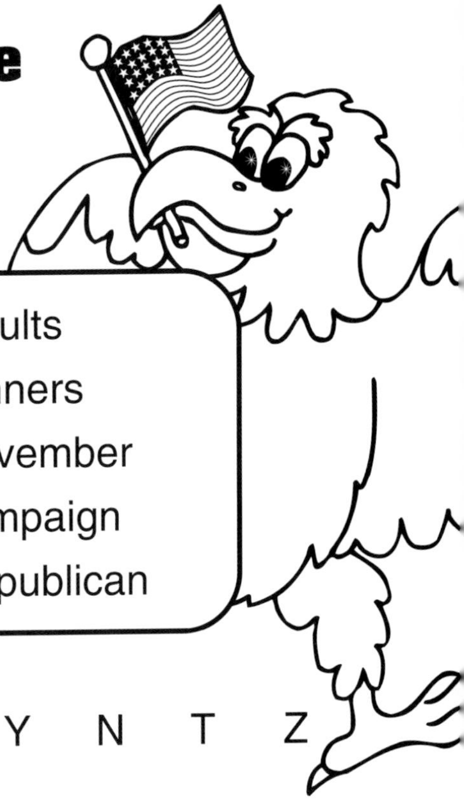

Look for the Election Day vocabulary words. Look across, up-and-down, and backwards. Cross off the words in the Word Bank as you find them.

Word Bank

machines	eighteen	results
vote	polls	winners
ballot	Tuesday	November
election	candidate	campaign
precinct	Democrat	Republican

```
T U E S D A Y O S E Y N T Z
U C I T N D W J B A L L O T
N A C M O E I P Y G X A T U
A M A F V R N H A I V O R T
C P N D E K N O F D O U P C
I A D I M B E L E C T I O N
L I I S B A R H N P E R L I
B G D O E L S Q L B W S L C
U N A G R L R E S U L T S E
P U T A R C O M E D M E I R
E P E I G H T E E N O I G P
R E M J M A C H I N E S T H
```

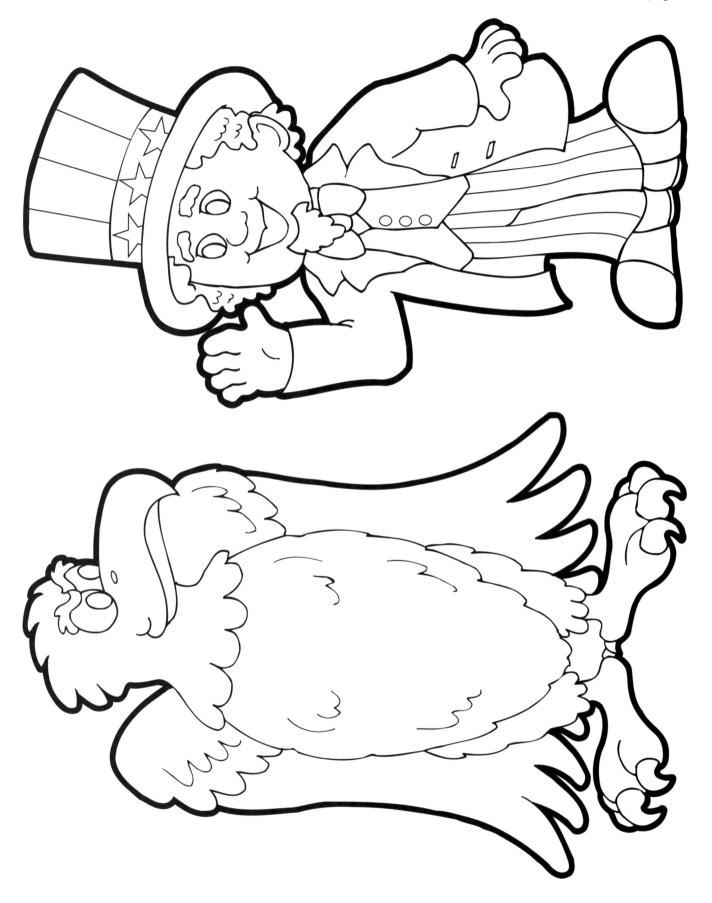

Patterns

Use with "Campaign Buttons" on page 19.

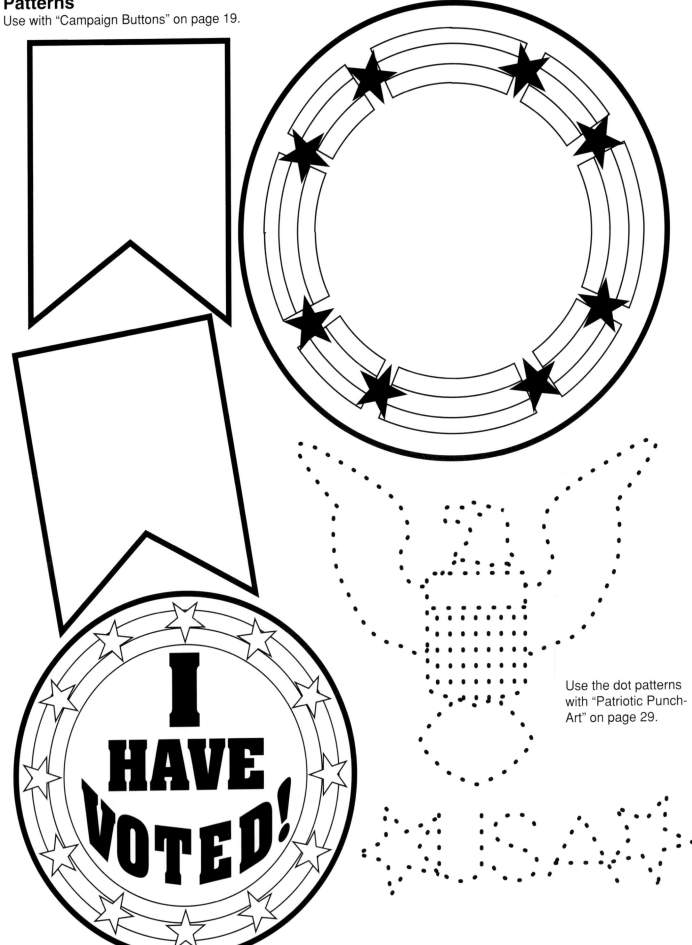

Use the dot patterns with "Patriotic Punch-Art" on page 29.

I HAVE VOTED!

Your House, My House—The White House!

Welcome your students to the White House! Share some fascinating facts and figures about the famous house where first families have lived for almost 200 years.

Ideas by Pam Kucks, Trish Pecuch, and Kathy Wolf

White House Wisdom

Challenge your classroom historians with trivia questions about the White House. Read aloud *The Story Of The White House* by Kate Waters (Scholastic Inc., 1991) and create this presidential bulletin board. Enlarge, color, and cut out the White House pattern on page 30. Cover your bulletin board with dark blue paper. Add the White House cutout and the title as shown. Create a border with white and red crepe-paper streamers or strips of white and red paper.

Cut out 32 paper circles from white paper. Write a partial trivia statement on one circle and the missing answer on another. Use pushpins to attach the 16 answer circles to the board as shown. Punch a hole in each of the fact circles and store them in a pocket on the board. The student picks a fact and hangs it on the pushpin above the correct answer. To make this activity self-checking, provide an answer key in the pocket.

1. The White House sits on _____ acres. *18*
2. When first built, the White House was known as the _____. *President's House*
3. The only president who didn't live in the White House was _____. *George Washington*
4. The man who designed the White House was _____. *James Hoban*
5. Building began on the White House in the year _____. *1792*
6. The first president to live in the White House was _____. *John Adams*
7. British soldiers set fire to the White House in _____. *1812*
8. The White House has _____ rooms. *132*
9. Abigail Adams hung _____ to dry in the East Room. *laundry*
10. The president conducts his business in the _____. *Oval Office*
11. One hundred forty people can be seated for dinner in the _____. *State Dining Room*
12. Press conferences are held in the biggest room, the _____. *East Room*
13. The president's helicopter lands on the _____. *South Lawn*
14. The address of the White House is _____ Pennsylvania Avenue. *1600*
15. The White House is located in _____. *Washington, DC*
16. The White House is home to a cat named _____. *Socks*

White House Interior Designers

Tell students that the White House was the biggest residence in America when it was built. As our country has grown, the Executive Mansion has grown—to 132 rooms! Each first family has added to the interior design and decoration of this special house. President Thomas Jefferson ordered wallpaper and furniture from France. President Franklin Roosevelt added an indoor swimming pool. President Dwight Eisenhower added a putting green to the White House lawn. And President John F. Kennedy's wife, Jackie, restored the mansion to its grandeur of the early 1800s.

For some creative thinking, give students the choice of designing a new room as an addition to the White House or redecorating a famous room such as the Lincoln Bedroom. Students may illustrate their new rooms or create collage-type posters by cutting and pasting pictures of furnishings from discarded home-decorating magazines. Since many of the rooms in the White House have special names, ask students to name their rooms too. Have students share their designs with the class; then put the rooms on display with labeled index cards that read, "Designed by [student's name]."

The Red Room
Designed by
John Hayes

The President's House Design Contest
Official Entry Form

1. Name _Donna Teal_
2. School _Collinsville Primary School_   Date _November 16, 1996_
3. School Address _254 South Elm Street_
   Collinsville, VA 24078
4. Grade _2_   Teacher _Miss Martin_

Describe the president's house and tell why the first family will like your house plans best:
They would feel safe because I would make all the glass bullet-proof.

The President's House Design Contest
Official Entry Form

1. Name _Barry Slate_   Date _November 16, 1996_
2. School _Collinsville Primary School_
3. School Address _254 South Elm Street_
   Collinsville, VA 24078
4. Grade _2_   Teacher _Miss Martin_

Winner

Describe the president's house and tell why the first family will like your house plans best:
They would like to live in my house because I would put a great big hot tub in there to relax in after a hard day of being the first family.

Executive Mansion Contest

Explain to your class that George Washington never lived in the White House. While Congress debated where to put the nation's capital, Washington lived in three different houses! When a site was finally chosen and it was time to build the president's house, a contest was held to pick the best house plans. A committee chose the house designed by a young Irish-American architect named James Hoban. Building began in 1792. President John Adams moved into the unfinished mansion in 1800. Over the years it has been added to many times.

For more creative thinking and writing practice, hold a class contest to design a new house for the president and his family. Invite your students to sketch plans and submit written descriptions on the official contest form on page 31. Display the plans. Choose an impartial committee to pick the three best designs and pin red, white, and blue ribbons on the winning entries. Reward all participants with cupcakes decorated with white frosting and red and blue sprinkles.

As your architects savor their rewards, announce that you are sending the winning designs to the president at 1600 Pennsylvania Avenue! Help students compose a class letter to enclose. What will the president think about his new Executive Mansion? Look for a reply in the mail.

Presidential Moments

For creative dramatics, create a White House setting in your classroom—the president's Oval Office! Help students find pictures of this famous room and re-create it with simple props; A table and chairs, a telephone, desk flags, a pen and paper, a potted plant, a U. S. flag, and a flag with the presidential seal are all that's needed. (See p.30.)

Then divide students into groups to act out scenes from the history of the Oval Office. Have older students research some of the famous people who have met in this room. Or have students use their imaginations to create scenes between past or recent presidents and world leaders, or famous sports and music stars. Here are some suggestions for starters:

- Dolley Madison telling the president that the British are coming
- President Lincoln meeting with his generals during the Civil War
- President Franklin Roosevelt telling the nation about Pearl Harbor
- President Kennedy meeting with Martin Luther King, Jr.
- Jackie Kennedy talking with other first ladies about redecorating
- President Nixon meeting with Elvis
- President Reagan offering jelly beans to Queen Elizabeth and George Washington
- President Washington meeting with the Dallas Cowboys
- President Clinton playing the sax with a rock group

The Oval Office

Mr. President

Have each group select a tour guide to set the stage with some background information about the characters and the year. Allow students to dress up and present their skits to parents. Be sure to take photos of these presidential moments to share.

An American Museum

Not only is the White House the home of the president and his family, but it's also a museum filled with priceless old furniture and irreplaceable gifts from foreign lands. Explain that the White House is a popular place for tourists visiting Washington, DC. Over 6,000 people visit the White House every day. The first family's private living quarters are on the second floor, so tourists can only visit five rooms on the first floor. Tours are conducted under tight security. Tourists cannot bring in food, drinks, or cameras. Chewing gum is also not allowed!

For some critical thinking, ask students to think of possible reasons for these strict rules. Then have students brainstorm a list of things they would like to see if they could tour the entire house.

Meet The President

To encourage creative writing, share the book *Arthur Meets The President* by Marc Brown (The Trumpet Club, 1991) with your class. Arthur wins a national writing contest with an essay on how he can help make America great. His whole class gets to visit Washington, DC, and attend a special ceremony at the White House. Arthur is nervous about reciting his essay for the president, but he gets a little help when the big moment arrives.

Ask students how they think Arthur felt when he met the president. How would your students feel? Invite your class to write essays about how they would make America great. Have students read their essays aloud as part of a patriotic celebration or on the school public address system.

Presidential Pets

Your students will be interested to hear that the White House has been the home of many first-family pets. Among them were a pet goat named Old Whiskers that belonged to President Benjamin Harrison's son and a pony named Macaroni that belonged to Caroline Kennedy. President Franklin Roosevelt seldom went anywhere without his beloved dog Fala. President Lyndon Johnson had two beagles named Him and Her. President George Bush's dog Millie had puppies in the White House. President Bill Clinton's family has a cat named Socks.

Share these fascinating facts about presidential pooches and pets. Then, to encourage some creative writing, have students pick the best pet for the president. First have each student draw a picture of his choice for the best pet or cut a picture from a magazine and mount it on construction paper. Then have each student write a paragraph telling why he thinks the president and his family should have this pet. Be sure to include instructions on caring for the new pet too. Allow students to name their pets and share their choices with the class. Have students vote for their top three choices of pets and record the results on a bar graph.

Patriotic Punch-Art

These punched-tin decorations have an Early American look that's perfect for displaying symbols of our country. You may want to recruit some parent volunteers since your students will be working with hammers and nails. Provide each student with a 5" x 5" piece of heavy tinfoil or the center cut from an aluminum pie plate. (Cut the pieces ahead of time and apply heavy masking tape around sharp edges to prevent cuts.) Duplicate the dot patterns on page 24 for students. Have each student choose a pattern. Demonstrate how to center and tape the dot pattern over the tin. Place an old magazine or thick layers of newspaper under the tin. Using a nail and small hammer, each student pounds the nail tip at each dot just enough to leave small holes in the tin. When he has punched holes around the entire pattern, he removes the paper and holds the tin up to a light to see the design. Use fabric binding, cardboard, or construction paper to frame each design as shown. Hang these patriotic symbols from the ceiling to add some punch to your White House studies!

Letters To Washington

For some letter-writing practice, have students write for information about the White House. Contact The Washington Convention and Visitors Association, 1400 Pennsylvania Avenue, Washington, DC 20004. Show students the correct form for a business letter and how to address an envelope. Display the responses and materials procured.

To culminate your unit on the White House, have students write letters to Washington—George Washington, that is. Ask students to tell ol' George what they learned about the White House. After all, he didn't get to see the White House completed!

Mrs. Robyn White
Delaney Avenue Elementary
P. O. Box 962
Greensboro NC 27412

32¢

The Washington Convention and
Visitors Association
1400 Pennsylvania Avenue
Washington DC 20004

Pattern

Use with "White House Wisdom" on page 25.

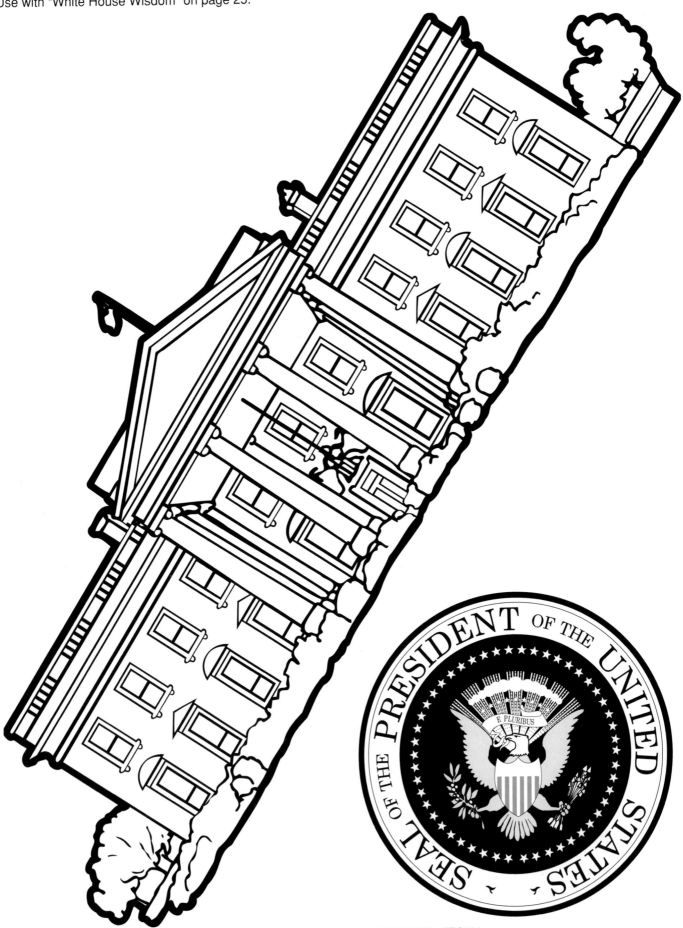

The President's House Design Contest
Official Entry Form

1. Name _____ Date _____

2. School _____

3. School Address _____

   _____

4. Grade _____ Teacher _____

Draw the president's house here:

Describe the president's house and tell why the first family will like your house plans best:

_____

_____

_____

Note To The Teacher: Use this reproducible with "Executive Mansion Contest" on page 26.

Name _____

Take A Tour With A White House Mouse

Wilbur The White House Mouse knows his way around the White House.
Take a tour with Wilbur. Read each sentence. Cut and paste each mouse to show where Wilbur went.

1. The **North Portico** faces Pennsylvania Avenue.
2. The president's **Oval Office** is in the West Wing.
3. The president's helicopter lands on the **South Lawn**.
4. The **East Wing** is where the president's military aides work.
5. News reporters use the **pressrooms** in the West Terrace.
6. The **private movie theater** in the East Terrace is for the president and his guests.

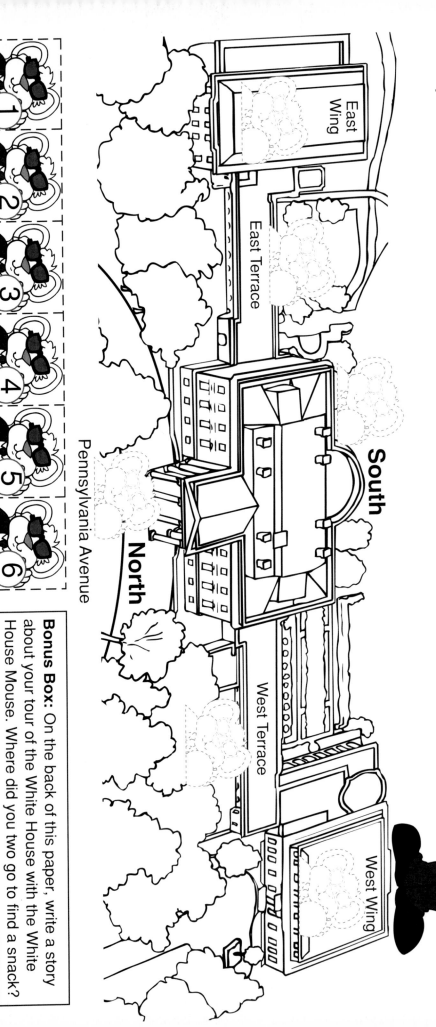

East Wing

East Terrace

South

North

Pennsylvania Avenue

West Terrace

West Wing

©1996 The Education Center, Inc. • NOVEMBER • TEC194

1 2 3 4 5 6

Bonus Box: On the back of this paper, write a story about your tour of the White House with the White House Mouse. Where did you two go to find a snack?

32

Marvelous Marc Brown

Celebrate Marc Brown's birthday on November 25 with Arthur and the gang!

by Resa Audet

Meet Marc Brown

As a child growing up in Pennsylvania, Marc Brown was very close to his grandmother, whom he credits with sparking his love of storytelling. His grandmother also nurtured his talent in art by providing him with materials, praise, and the means for going to art school.

After working at a variety of jobs—such as truck driving, acting, chicken farming, and teaching—Brown began to illustrate children's books. His first book, *Arthur's Nose,* was based on a bedtime story that he created for his first son, Tolon. Since then Marc Brown and his lovable character, Arthur, have both developed quite a few fans. In fact, Arthur has his own fan club! Students (or a class) can join the Arthur Fan Club for one dollar. Send your name, address, age, and a self-addressed, stamped envelope to:

Little, Brown and Company
c/o The Arthur Fan Club
34 Beacon Street
Boston, MA 02108-1493

Arthur's Pet Business

(Joy Street Books, 1990)

Arthur begins a pet-care business to prove that he is responsible enough to own a puppy. Soon Arthur's house begins to resemble a zoo! After reading this madcap adventure aloud, have each student do some creative thinking and draw a picture of the animals that he would take care of if he owned a pet-care business. Below the illustration, have each student describe how he would take care of the pets. Ask each child how he would advertise his business and how much he would charge for his services. Have students design posters or business cards to advertise their pet businesses. Your young business owners are sure to profit from this activity!

Arthur's Teacher Trouble

(Joy Street Books, 1989)

Spark interest in spelling by reading *Arthur's Teacher Trouble.* In this story, Arthur enters and wins the school spelling bee. Ask students why they think Arthur won the competition. Emphasize the fact that Arthur gave up some of his playtime to study. Point out that Arthur's family helped him a great deal, also.

Have students use some of these pointers to prepare for a class spelling bee. Give each student a list of spelling words to study. In addition to having students practice their words at home, provide time in class for student pairs to study together. After the spelling bee, give each participant a copy of the "Super Speller" award on page 37. Arthur may be just the inspiration your students need to soar in spelling!

The True Francine
(Joy Street Books, 1987)

Francine learns a valuable lesson about friendship when her good friend Muffy lets her take the blame for cheating on a test. Help students gain valuable insights about friendship while practicing oral communication skills. Read the story aloud; then discuss Muffy's actions throughout the story. Was Muffy a good friend at the beginning of the story? In the middle of the story? At the end of the story? After discussing the story, invite students to hold a friendship forum.

Have students sit in a large circle. Encourage each student to tell why he is a good friend; then invite students to take turns discussing the value of friendship and the qualities of good friends. Your students will soon be teaching Muffy a thing or two about friendship!

Arthur's Birthday
(Little, Brown and Company; 1991)

Celebrate Marc Brown's birthday—and Arthur's, too—by reading *Arthur's Birthday*. Arthur's friends are excited about his upcoming birthday party until they discover that it is scheduled for the same day as Muffy's party. Leave it to Arthur to figure out the perfect solution!

Make Arthur's birthday really special by baking a cake for your class to share. Have students design festive birthday cards for Arthur or Marc Brown. You may wish to send these cards to Marc Brown at the following address:

Marc Brown
Little, Brown and Company
34 Beacon Street
Boston, MA 02108-1493

Arthur Babysits
(Joy Street Books, 1992)

When Arthur is asked to babysit for Mrs. Tibble, he begins to worry. Will he be able to manage the terrible Tibble twins? Before you read aloud the conclusion to this story, ask students to brainstorm ways that Arthur can encourage the twins to behave. Record students' ideas on a chart. After you read the story, have students list the qualities of a good babysitter. Discuss the types of things that a babysitter should know and be able to do in order to take good care of her charges.

Then divide your class into groups and provide a copy of page 36 for each group. Have each group program the page with child-care instructions and safety rules that a good babysitter should follow. Invite groups of students to share their work aloud; then bind the pages into a book titled "The Babysitting Instruction Manual." Your future babysitters will learn a lot by browsing through this informative book.

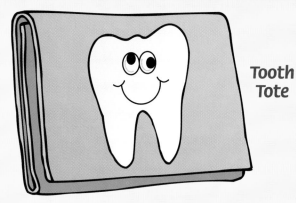

Tooth Tote

Arthur's Tooth

(Little, Brown and Company; 1986)

Arthur is disappointed that he is the only one in his class who hasn't lost a baby tooth. All of his friends have suggestions for solving the problem, but the actual solution takes Arthur completely by surprise! After sharing this story with your class, invite a dentist to speak with youngsters about the development and care of teeth. Then involve each student in making a special Tooth Tote for storing lost teeth.

Each child will need a 4" x 9" strip of colored felt, a 2 1/2" white construction-paper square, a tooth template, a 1" square of self-adhesive Velcro®, scissors, crayons or markers, and craft glue. To make a Tooth Tote, fold up the bottom third of the felt strip; then glue the sides to create a pocket. Fold down the top third of the felt to make a flap; then create a fastener by attaching Velcro® to the pocket and to the inside of the flap. Trace and cut out a construction-paper tooth. Glue small wiggle eyes to the tooth if desired; then glue the tooth to the front of the tote flap. This Tooth Tote will keep each child's precious tooth safe until the pouch is placed under a pillow to await the Tooth Fairy's visit!

Arthur's Eyes

(Joy Street Books, 1986)

Arthur's poor eyesight makes him feel bad, but the teasing he endures when he gets eyeglasses makes him feel worse. Use this story to prompt a discussion of the importance of good vision. Ask students to list the pros and cons of wearing glasses. Invite students who wear glasses to share their experiences of getting and wearing them. Then show students that eyeglasses are clearly cool by making these bespectacled self-portraits.

Each child will need a 9" x 12" sheet of white construction paper, colorful fabric and construction-paper scraps, scissors, glue, and a variety of craft materials such as beads, glitter, and sequins. Have each child draw and decorate her likeness on the sheet of white construction paper. Using a variety of craft materials, have each child create a spectacular pair of spectacles to add to her picture. Mount these eye-catching projects on a bulletin board titled "Eyeglasses Are Out-Of-Sight!"

More Great Books By Marc Brown

Arthur's Chicken Pox
Published by Little, Brown and Company; 1994

Arthur's Nose
Published by Joy Street Books, 1986

D.W. All Wet
Published by Little, Brown and Company; 1991

D.W. The Picky Eater
Published by Little, Brown and Company; 1995

The Bionic Bunny Show
Published by Joy Street Books, 1985

Dinosaurs To The Rescue: A Guide To Protecting Our Planet
Published by Little, Brown and Company; 1994

Note To Teacher:
Use with *"Arthur Babysits"* on page 34.

Name _____

Babysitting Instruction Manual

A Good Babysitter Always...

A Good Babysitter Never...

Indoor Fun

Outdoor Fun

Prepare For Emergencies

Great Books To Read Aloud:

is a
Super Speller!

Signed _____

Date _____

Bookmark

Places! You Take Can Reading

A Fabulous Fowl—The Turkey

You can hardly think of November without this famous fowl coming to mind. But give the poor old gobbly-wobbly bird a break from the traditional holiday meal. Concentrate on having some fowl fun while reinforcing basic skills!

Ideas by Trish Pecuch

Turkey Fact Or Fiction

They know he's usually the center of attention on Thanksgiving, but what else do your students know about Tom Turkey? Create a fact vs. fiction game with the facts below. Duplicate 20 feathers (see the pattern on page 42) on colored construction paper. Cut out the feathers. Write one fact on each feather. Program each of the remaining eight feathers with false statements about turkeys. Laminate the feathers, if desired, and place them in a box. Place the box of feathers at a center with an answer key for individual review.

Then invite students to separate the turkey facts from fiction. Have a student pick a feather, read the sentence, and tell if it is true or false. Place the fact feathers in one pile and the fiction feathers in another.

Turkey Facts:
- Male turkeys are called *toms*.
- Female turkeys are called *hens*.
- Young turkeys are called *poults*.
- The long piece of loose skin hanging beneath the turkey's lower jaw is called a *wattle*.
- A tom's *beard* is a tuft of stiff feathers on his breast.
- Many domestic turkeys have white or light-colored feathers.
- Wild turkeys have brown or bronze-tipped feathers.
- Wild turkeys usually weigh only about ten pounds.
- Only wild turkeys can fly.
- Wild turkeys rest in trees at night.
- Turkey eggs are tan with brown specks.
- Turkey eggs are twice as big as chicken eggs.

Campaigning For Mr. Turkey

Did you know that when our founding fathers met to choose a national symbol, Benjamin Franklin wanted to make the turkey our national bird? After discussing this bit of historical trivia, have students tell why they think the bald eagle was chosen instead of the turkey. For some creative writing, have students write letters to the editor of your local newspaper supporting the turkey as our national bird. How convincing can they be about the virtues of this fabulous fowl? Have students share their letters and send them to the newspaper for possible publication!

A Feather In Your Cap

Looking for ways to put a feather in your cap? Here are a few creative ways to use feathers in November:

• Write a special message such as "I'm thankful you're in my class!" on feather cutouts. Laminate them and present one to each child as a special holiday bookmark.

• Use real feathers (available at craft stores) as rewards or tokens. Or duplicate the award on page 42 and tape a real feather to it before presenting it to each child.

• Create a bulletin-board turkey and add feather cutouts for good behavior or good work.

• Use feather cutouts as nonstandard units of measure. Let children measure objects in your classroom and record the number of feathers on a chart.

• Keep a supply of feather cutouts handy and use them to introduce new vocabulary words or math facts. Or use them as nametags or hall passes.

One, Two, Gobble, Four

Here's a challenging counting game to use as a five-minute filler while waiting in line or for an activity to begin. Cut out nine turkey feathers and number them one to nine. (See the pattern on page 42.) Turn the numbers over and have a student choose one number to start the game. The chosen numeral becomes the "gobble" number. Whenever the number or a multiple of the number is reached in counting, the student must say "Gobble!" instead of the number. If a student says the number instead of the gobble number, the counting must start over. Increase the difficulty by using two gobble numbers at a time. Happy gobbling!

Fashionable Fowl

Mr. Turkey is known for strutting his stuff. Have students create these Fashion Turkeys to strut across your bulletin board. Duplicate the patterns on page 43 for each student to cut out. Have students trace the body, head, and wattle pieces on colored construction paper and glue as shown. Students can cut out feet and a beak from paper scraps and glue these features to their turkeys. Next, students trace their tail-feather patterns on fancy wallpaper samples and cut them out. Demonstrate how to glue the tail-feather piece and make cuts in it to look like ruffled feathers. Students can add other details to personalize their birds. How about a fashionable pair of shoes or boots from an old catalog?

Have each student copy the poem below and fill in the blank with two or more words that describe the color or pattern on his turkey's tail. Display the turkeys and poems on your bulletin board with the title "Fashionable Fowl." Which turkey makes the best fashion statement for the holidays? Have students vote for the best-dressed bird in town!

Mr. Fashion Turkey
Your colors are so bright—
With _____ tail feathers,
You really are a sight!

Mr. Fashion Turkey
Your colors are so bright—
With purple flower tail feathers,
You really are a sight!

Step On The Scales!

For some practice in estimating weight, have students compare frozen turkeys to familiar items! Ask each student to find out how large the turkey will be on his family's dinner table and write this weight on a slip of paper. Place all the slips in a paper bag. Provide items for comparison, such as a one-pound weight or bag of birdseed, a five-pound bag of sugar, a ten-pound bag of potatoes, and a 20-pound frozen turkey. Have students sequence the items by weight. Then have each student pull a paper slip from the bag. Have the student put enough weight in a shopping bag to equal the weight of the turkey on the slip. Provide a scale for students to check their efforts. Ask students how many 20-pound turkeys it would take to equal an average third grader or maybe even the teacher—if you don't mind sharing your weight!

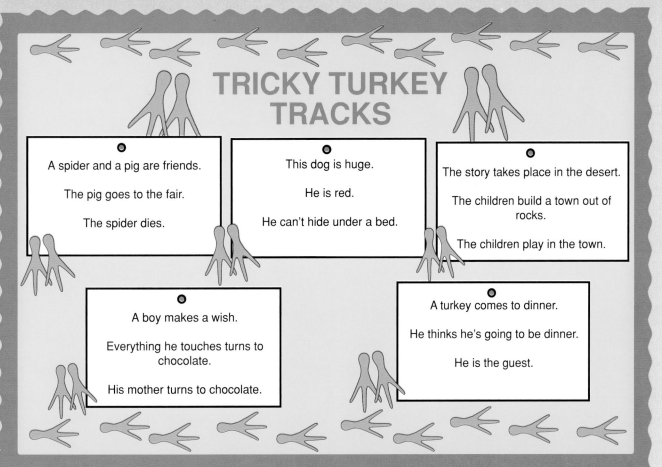

TRICKY TURKEY TRACKS

A spider and a pig are friends.

The pig goes to the fair.

The spider dies.

This dog is huge.

He is red.

He can't hide under a bed.

The story takes place in the desert.

The children build a town out of rocks.

The children play in the town.

A boy makes a wish.

Everything he touches turns to chocolate.

His mother turns to chocolate.

A turkey comes to dinner.

He thinks he's going to be dinner.

He is the guest.

Tricky Turkey Tracks

Students can track down good books with this reading incentive display! Cover your bulletin board with yellow background paper. Duplicate the track patterns on page 42 for students to color and cut out. Make a border of turkey tracks and add the title "Tricky Turkey Tracks."

As each child completes a good book, have him write his name, the title, and the author one side of an index card. On the other side, have him write three clues to the title of the book. Punch a hole in the top of the index card. The child adds his index card to the board by hanging it on a pushpin with the clue side up. Beside his clue card he pins a pair of tracks. Students read the descriptions and turn the cards over to discover the book's title and who made the tracks.

To vary this bulletin board, display students' papers with track cutouts. Add the title "Trackin' Down Good Work!"

Patterns

Use with "Turkey Fact Or Fiction" on page 38, and "One, Two, Gobble, Four" and "A Feather In Your Cap" on page 39.

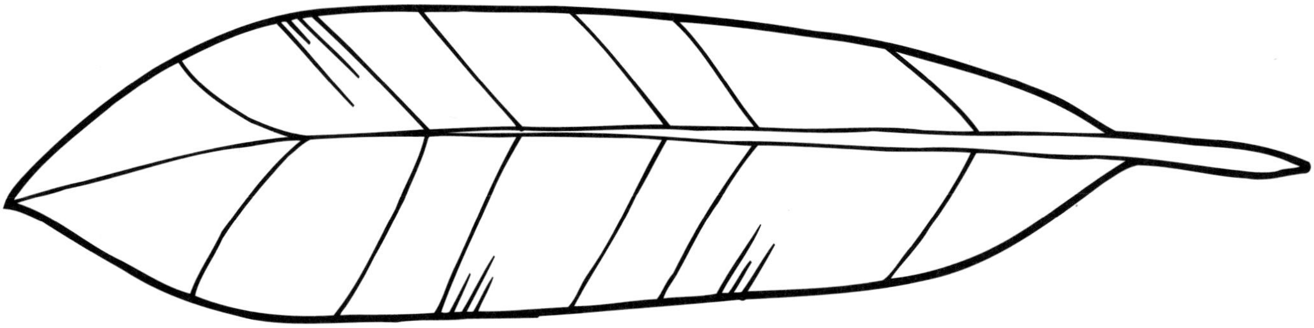

Use with "Tricky Turkey Tracks" on page 41.

Award

Use with "A Feather In Your Cap" on page 39.

_____,

Here's A Feather In Your Cap

for

_____

_____

_____ !

Keep Up The Good Work!

Teacher _____ Date_____

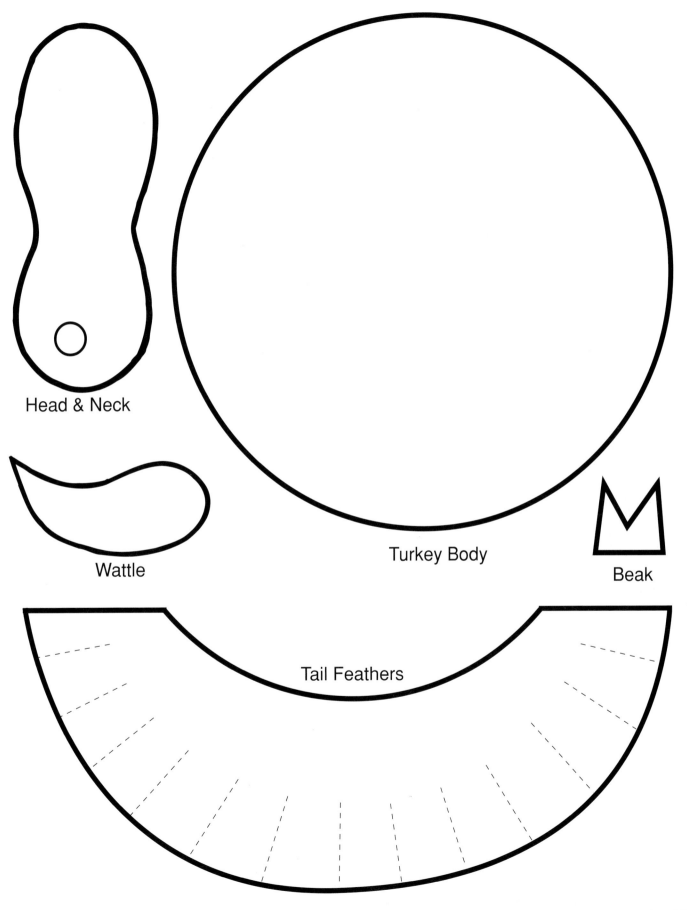

Head & Neck

Wattle

Turkey Body

Beak

Tail Feathers

Name _____

Let's Talk Turkey

Write the words on each feather in ABC order on the turkey next to it.
Look at the second and third letters to help you.

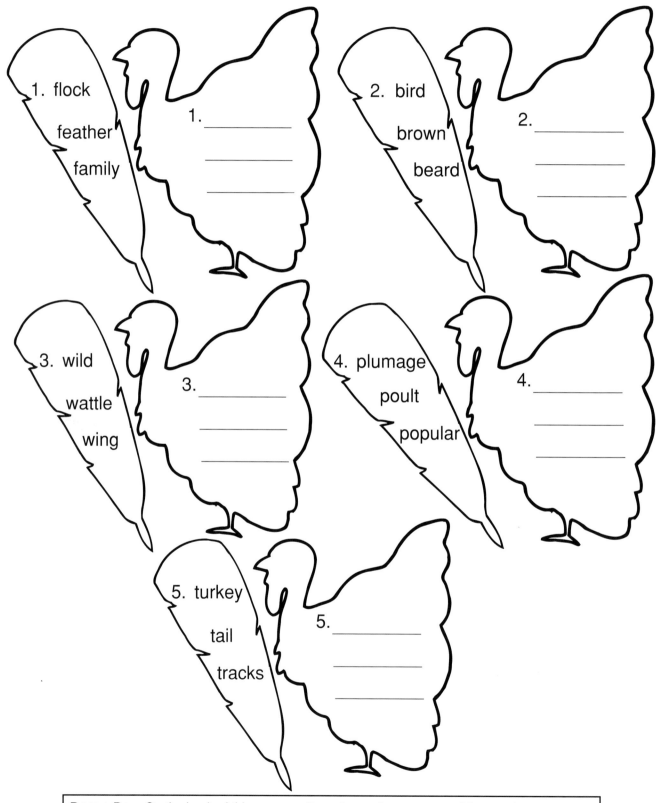

1. flock
   feather
   family

1. _____
   _____
   _____

2. bird
   brown
   beard

2. _____
   _____
   _____

3. wild
   wattle
   wing

3. _____
   _____
   _____

4. plumage
   poult
   popular

4. _____
   _____
   _____

5. turkey
   tail
   tracks

5. _____
   _____
   _____

Bonus Box: On the back of this paper, write a story using as many of the words as you can.

Travelin' Turkeys

Follow the traveling turkeys on a map of the United States.
Write the answers in each blank.

1. Tonya Turkey ran from New York to California. What direction did she travel? _____
2. Terry Turkey took a bus from Florida to Maine. What direction did he travel? _____
3. Tammy and Teresa Turkey took a train from Texas to Tennessee. What direction did they travel? _____
4. Mr. and Mrs. Turkey live in Ohio. They took a vacation on a turkey ranch in North Carolina. What direction did they travel? _____
5. Mr. Tom Turkey hightailed it out of Texas heading north. What state did he come to first? _____
6. Ima Turkey visits her aunt in Florida every winter. Ima lives in Georgia. What direction must she travel to get there? _____
7. Tabitha Turkey flew east from North Carolina. What ocean did she reach? _____
8. Mr. Tom Turkey ran from the United States to Mexico. What direction did he run? _____
9. If Tyler Turkey lived in New York and strutted directly north, what country would he be in? _____
10. Toby Turkey's paper route takes him from Nebraska to South Dakota. What direction does he travel? _____
11. Tessie Turkey flew one state west to see her sister in Vermont. In what state does Tessie live? _____
12. Tucker Turkey flew from Canada to the United States. What direction did he fly? _____

A Feast Full Of
Thanksgiving Ideas

Here's a cornucopia of ideas to help you incorporate skills with your Thanksgiving festivities.

Ideas by Nancy Matthews

Welcome To America!

Today, when reflecting on Thanksgiving, students think of turkey dinners, Thanksgiving Day parades, football games, and family and friends coming together. Explore some of the similarities and differences between Thanksgiving today and Thanksgiving centuries ago by reading *Thanksgiving Day* by Gail Gibbons (Holiday House, Inc.; 1983) to your students. This is a short story about the origin of Thanksgiving and how it is celebrated today. Summarize the story by telling students that the Pilgrims sailed from England to America to find a new life with religious freedom. The Pilgrims were met by Indians who lived in the area. At first, they were suspicious of each other. But the Indians taught the Pilgrims how to plant, hunt, and gather food. After their first harvest, the Pilgrims were thankful for a bountiful crop and for the help of the Indians in producing it. They invited the Indians to celebrate with them in the first Thanksgiving feast.

Compare the two cultures by having students think of ways the guests were different from their Pilgrim hosts. Some examples are clothing, language, appearance, eating habits, and skills. Divide the class into two groups. Have students in each group imagine they are either Pilgrims or Indians. Have each group tell what its thoughts or suspicions might be about the other group. Ask students to compare these fears to how they think a new student might feel in a new school. Together list ways that students might make new students feel welcome. Wrap up with a discussion about how we can help people from other lands feel welcome in America today.

A Bountiful Basket

Most of us are fortunate enough to enjoy a Thanksgiving feast. Remind students to be thankful for the food on their tables with this class project. At the beginning of your unit on Thanksgiving and continuing until the holiday, encourage students to think of those less fortunate by bringing in food for the needy. First decide as a class who will benefit from the collection. Students can prepare a holiday basket for a needy family, or they may choose a church or homeless shelter to receive their Thanksgiving gift. Encourage students to bring in canned fruits and vegetables; canned or bottled juices; bags of rice, raisins, and nuts; etc. Students may supplement the basket by bringing in spare change to buy a turkey for the recipient of the gift. No rewards or incentives should be given to students who participate. The good feeling of giving is reward enough.

Living In Plymouth Colony

Students learn about the Pilgrim houses of Plymouth Colony by reading the books *Oh, What A Thanksgiving!* by Steven Kroll (Scholastic Inc., 1988) and *Sarah Morton's Day* by Kate Waters (Scholastic Inc., 1989). Point out the illustrations and reproductions of houses of the 1620s, and discuss how they compare to the houses of today. The typical Pilgrim cottage was a small, one-room shelter made of wooden posts covered by sticks and straw mixed with clay. Wooden clapboards were used on well-to-do homes. Each cottage had a steep, thatched roof and a chimney made of clay and sticks.

To make a Pilgrim cottage, provide a clean, empty, half-pint milk carton for each child. Cut lengths of craft sticks to glue to all sides of the milk carton. After students glue on their clapboards, help them cover the roofs. Paint the top of each carton with a layer of thick white glue. Dip each roof into a bowl of crumbled shredded wheat cereal to cover as shown. Next have each student glue on doors, windows, and a chimney cut from brown construction paper. Display the cottages in a village arrangement atop a table. Label the display "Plimoth Plantation," after the living-history museum in Plymouth, Massachusetts.

chimney

Sail With The *Mayflower*

The Pilgrims fled from England to find religious freedom. One hundred two passengers traveled across the ocean on a ship called the *Mayflower*. Share *The First Thanksgiving* by John Craighead George (Philomel Books, 1993) with students and then discuss the conditions the Pilgrims had to endure on their journey. Have students imagine they are passengers on the Mayflower and tell what they like or dislike about the voyage.

Make individual models of the *Mayflower* for creative dramatics. Enlarge the pattern on page 53 and duplicate a copy for each student on tagboard. Provide students with markers and crayons to decorate their ships. Cut out each ship and tape two 18-inch pieces of yarn or heavy string parallel to each other across the back of the ship cutout. Have each student tie the *Mayflower* around his waist and dramatize a scene from the journey.

Fish And Fertilizer

The Indians of Plymouth taught the Pilgrims how to plant corn the Indian way. They put a dead fish in the ground with the seeds to make the soil richer. Although foul-smelling, the decaying fish provided nutrients for the soil and resulted in a bountiful harvest for the Pilgrims. Ask students if anyone has a family garden or compost pile in the backyard. Have students find out why gardeners may prefer this natural fertilizer to chemical fertilizers. Explain that when chemicals are sprayed on plants, the chemicals can get into the water or harm animals.

A Quilt Made For Thanksgiving

Display students' thankfulness for all to see with this quilted bulletin board. Distribute a construction-paper square to each student. Instruct each child to write one thing that he is most thankful for in a complete sentence. Encourage each student to illustrate his piece of the quilt. Around the perimeter of the construction-paper square, use a black marker and a straight edge to make a broken line that represents stitches. Assemble and staple all pieces of the quilt together on the board. Add a border of gathered crepe streamers or inexpensive lace. Add the title "For This, We Give Thanks." Allow each student an opportunity to share his piece of the quilt with the class.

When the Thanksgiving holiday is over and the bulletin board is taken down, have students frame their quilt squares to take home. Cut a frame from an empty cereal box. Flip the frame over so the plain side shows. Cover the illustrated square with plastic wrap and tape it to the back side of the frame. Students take home their framed quilt squares to share with their families.

Gobblin' Good Vocabulary

 Brainstorm vocabulary words that have a Thanksgiving theme to use with a week full of tasks. Write the words on feather cutouts and mount them along with three turkeys, on the bulletin board as shown. (See the patterns on page 54.) Add the title, "Gobblin' Good Words." Place a shoebox and a roasting pan nearby. Students use the words to complete the following daily tasks:

• Choose a word from the board and come up with other Thanksgiving words that begin with each of its letters.

Ex: **G**iving
    Others
    Berries
    Bread
    Love
    Eating

• Write the words in ABC order.
• Write and illustrate a story about the turkey that came to your house for dinner. Use as many of the words as possible.
• Look up one word in the dictionary and write it on a feather cutout. Write its definition on another feather cutout. Put the feathers in the shoebox near the board. After all your classmates have contributed to the shoebox, take turns matching definitions to vocabulary words.
• Use as many words from the display as possible to create a word-search puzzle. Put your puzzle in the roasting pan. Once the pan is full of puzzles from the class, choose one and solve it.

Mmmm! Mmmm! Math

 This activity includes a little homework over Thanksgiving as well as a follow-up class math activity. Explain that the majority of families serve turkey for Thanksgiving dinner. Discuss the average size of turkeys. Guide the students to understand that the more people who will be sharing a Thanksgiving meal together, the bigger the turkey will probably be. Have each student estimate how many people will be eating Thanksgiving dinner with his family. Next have each student estimate how much their turkey will weigh. Over the holiday, have each student find out the actual weight of the turkey and count how many people are at the Thanksgiving celebration.

After the holiday, have students compile this information for a class math activity. Write all the students' names on the board or on a transparency. Give each student the opportunity to record his information about the turkey's actual weight and number of people. Then each student compares the actual and estimated weights of his turkey to find out how close the estimation was. Then repeat this process with the number of people. Who had the biggest turkey? The most people? Was it the same person?

49

Let's Talk Turkey–Books That Is!

Hungry for some holiday humor? Check out these books about turkeys!

'Twas The Night Before Thanksgiving
by Dav Pilkey
(Orchard Books, 1990)

Share this rhyming book based on "The Night Before Christmas" and have students compare the two stories. In Pilkey's tale, the lives of eight chunky turkeys are saved by students on a field trip to Farmer Mack Nuggett's turkey farm. After sharing the story, brainstorm with students foods other than turkey that can be served for a wonderful Thanksgiving feast.

For more creative thinking, instruct students to write a Thanksgiving menu for a restaurant that serves no turkey. Have students print their menus on unlined paper. Provide colored construction paper to make menu covers and glue the menus inside. For a decorative touch, provide yarn tassels and attach them as shown. Display the menus on a bulletin board titled "Hold The Turkey, Please!"

A Turkey For Thanksgiving
by Eve Bunting
(Clarion Books, 1991)

Share the humorous book *A Turkey For Thanksgiving* with students and follow up with creative writing. In this story, Turkey is invited to be a guest for a Thanksgiving feast at Mr. and Mrs. Moose's house. He avoids the invitation for fear that *he* will be Thanksgiving dinner. After sharing the story, have students imagine that they are turkeys and it is the day before Thanksgiving. Help students write stories from the point of view of a turkey on Thanksgiving Eve. Bind the writings into a class book titled "Mr. Turkey's Thanksgiving Eve Diary."

The Squirrels' Thanksgiving
by Steven Kroll
(Holiday House, Inc.; 1991)

After listening to this story, students will be more appreciative of their families. In *The Squirrel's Thanksgiving*, a brother and sister squirrel begin to appreciate each other after sharing Thanksgiving with their not-so-appreciative cousins. This story emphasizes the real meaning of Thanksgiving by encouraging youngsters to be thankful for their friends, families, and homes. After sharing this story, have students write notes to family members telling them why they are thankful for them. Tell students to slip the notes under the plates at Thanksgiving dinner and make someone's day!

Arthur's Thanksgiving

by Marc Brown

(Little, Brown and Co., 1983)

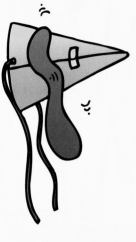

Share the story *Arthur's Thanksgiving* and let your students be turkeys for a day. In this story, Arthur is the director of the Thanksgiving play, but he can't find anyone to be the turkey. At the end of the story, everyone comes out on stage dressed like a turkey.

Create a turkey disguise for each student to strut around in. Distribute yellow and red construction paper, scissors, tape, and yarn to each student. The student draws a large half-circle on yellow paper and cuts it out. Roll the paper into a cone shape to make a beak and tape it as shown. Next each student draws a wattle on red paper, cuts it out, and tapes it to the top of the beak. Punch two holes as shown and tie on yarn pieces. Students place the beaks over their noses and tie behind their heads. Gobble! Gobble! Time for some turkey comedy!

More Thanksgiving Books

- *Silly Tilly's Thanksgiving Dinner* by Lillian Hoban (Harper Collins, 1990)
- *The First Thanksgiving* by Linda Hayward (Random House, Inc.; 1990)
- *It's Thanksgiving* by Jack Prelutsky (Greenwillow Books, 1982)
- *Daisy's Crazy Thanksgiving* by Margery Cuyler (Henry Holt And Company, 1990)
- *1, 2, 3 Thanksgiving!* by W. Nikola-Lisa (Albert Whitman And Co., 1991)
- *Thanksgiving At Our House* by Wendy Watson (Clarion Books, 1991)

Thanksgiving In The Classroom

To culminate your unit, prepare for a classroom Thanksgiving feast.

The Feast

 Discuss with students the meal that the Pilgrims and Indians shared in the 1620s. The fare consisted of wild turkey, lobster, goose, venison, onions, pumpkins, and corn bread. Together plan a menu for your classroom feast and list the items on a chart. Assign each student an item to bring for the feast. Menus will vary but may include foods such as apple or cranberry juice, turkey sandwiches from a deli, carrots, apples, instant pudding, or fruit salad. Remember to assign plates, silverware, cups, and napkins. Use the form on page 55 to send a reminder home to parents.

A Horn Of Plenty

 Share with students the book *Thanksgiving Day* by Gail Gibbons (Holiday House, Inc.; 1983). Point out that the horn of plenty mentioned in the story is also known as a *cornucopia*. The cornucopia is a symbol of Thanksgiving. Display a cornucopia and demonstrate how to arrange real fruits and vegetables inside it.

Provide students with the supplies to make miniature cornucopias to decorate their tables at the classroom feast. Distribute a sugar waffle cone to each student and instruct him to glue it on its side to a piece of construction paper. While this dries, discuss with students the fruits, vegetables, and nuts that are often seen in cornucopias. Give students time to create various fruits and vegetables from play dough. Place the sculpted foods in the cornucopias. Nuts in the shell can be added to the assortment. Place these decorations on the table at feast time.

Turkey Napkin Rings

Create these colorful turkey napkin rings for your classroom feast. Distribute a sheet of white construction paper, scissors, crayons or markers, glue, and one-half of an empty toilet-paper tube to student. Instruct the student to trace her hand on the construction paper and cut out the shape. Then have her color the fingers different colors to represent the feathers of the tail. Glue this to one side of the cardboard ring.

Duplicate the head pattern on page 55 for each student to color and cut out. Draw on two eyes and a beak. Glue the completed head opposite the tail feathers. Roll the napkin from corner to corner and insert it in the napkin ring. Students will want to take these turkeys home to use again.

Thoughts Of Thankfulness

 Now that the menu is planned and the table is decorated, it is time to remember the true meaning of Thanksgiving. Discuss with students things that they and you are thankful for today. Family, friends, food, health, and shelter may be some of them. Distribute a piece of writing paper to each student. Help students write poems that describe what they are thankful for. Have each student tape his poem to the underside of his plate. Set aside a moment before the feast for students to read their poems silently or aloud. (If a class feast is not planned, students can take their poem home for the holidays and read them to their family prior to Thanksgiving dinner.)

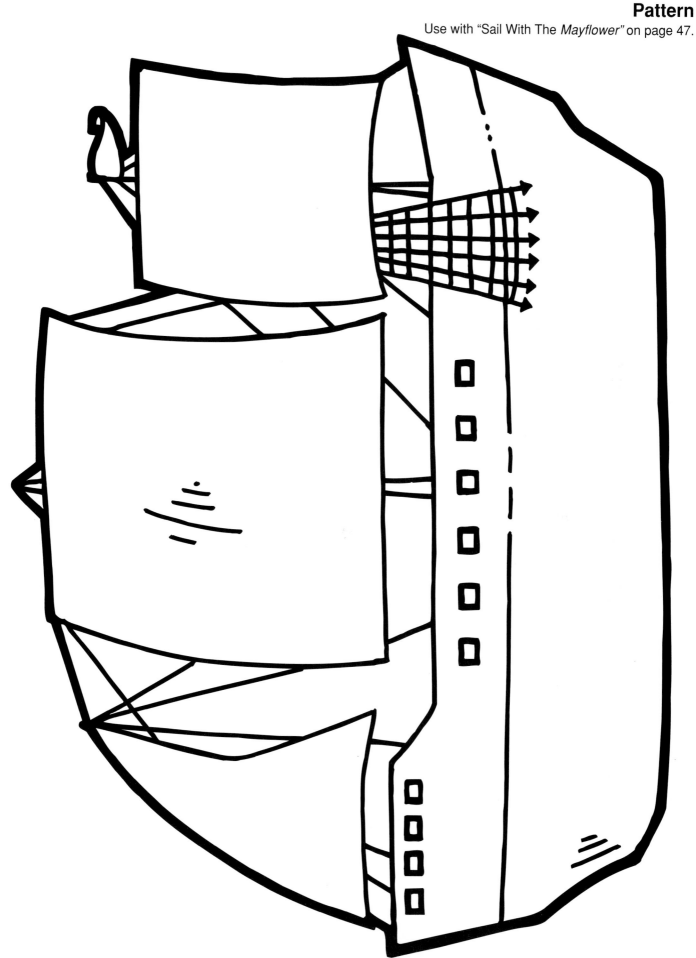

Patterns

Use with "Gobblin' Good Vocabulary" on page 49.

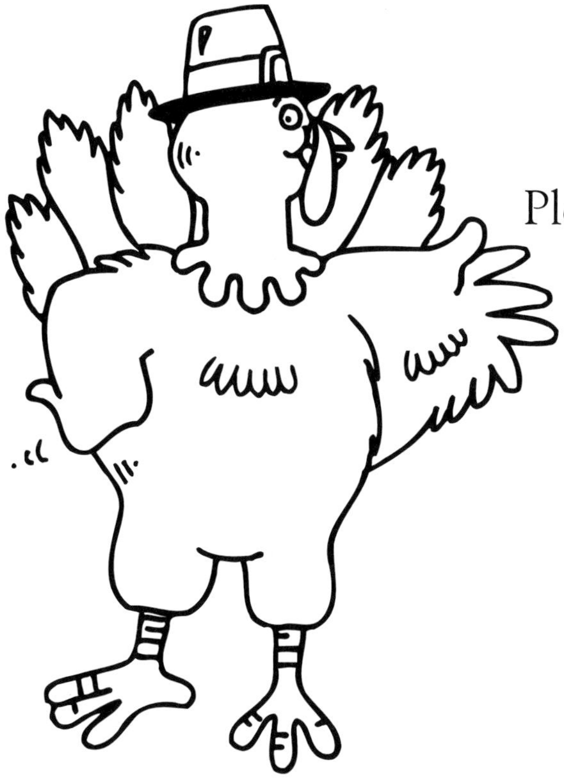

Gobble, gobble!
We need your help.

Please help us prepare for a classroom Thanksgiving Feast.

Date _____

Time _____

We need the following items:

Please sign and return this form by _____.

Name _____ Date _____

Pattern
Use with "Turkey Napkin Rings" on page 52.

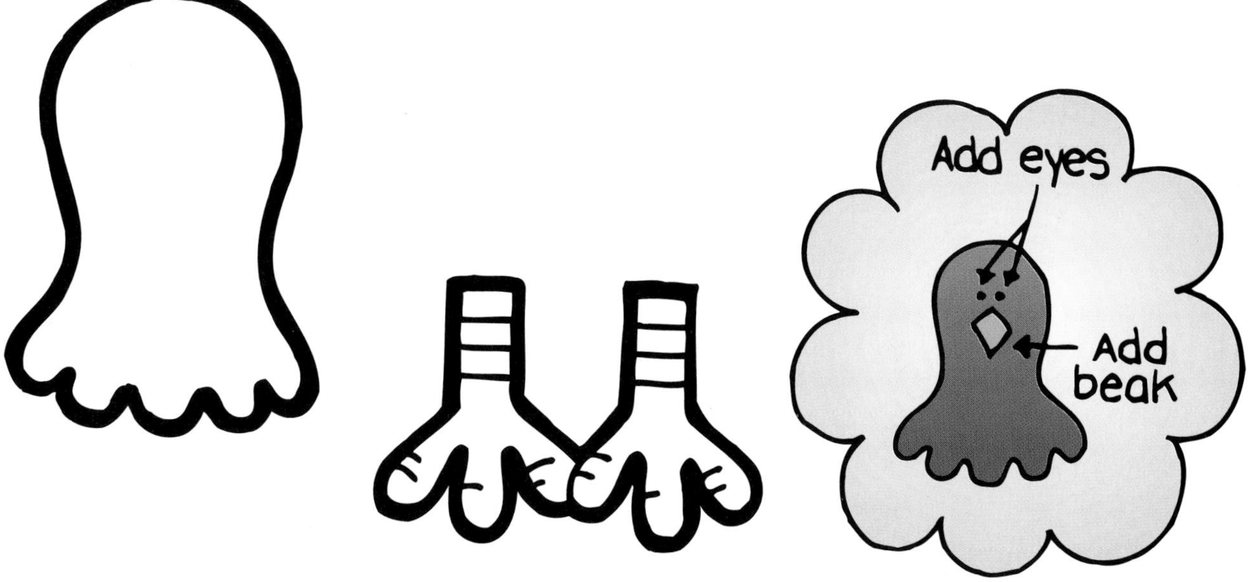

Add eyes

Add beak

The Iroquois

November means studying about Native Americans in many classrooms. The tie-in to Thanksgiving is a natural one. However, the study of the first Americans has gone in a more meaningful and accurate direction beyond the traditional week of Pilgrims and Indians. Rather than concentrating on the Eastern Woodland Indians of the first Thanksgiving, try introducing your students to the lifestyles of the Iroquois, Sioux, Navajo, *and* Tlingit peoples. As your students compare cultures, they will come to understand that each Native American culture is unique and has contributed to us in special ways.

Ideas by Resa Audet and Kathy Wolf

Six tribes—the Mohawk, the Oneida, the Onondaga, the Seneca, the Cayuga, and the Tuscarora—united long ago to form the Iroquois League. To introduce this culture to your students, display a bark basket if possible and ask students to determine what material it is made of and what might be carried in it. Explain that the Iroquois people were Eastern Woodland Indians who depended upon the resources of the rivers, lakes, and forests for survival. Write the following facts on sentence strips and share them with the class. Divide your class into groups and have each group create a display to illustrate one of the concepts. Give each group a choice of doing a diorama, map, mural, demonstration, or museum display.

— The Iroquois lived around the lakes and rivers in what is now New York State.
— The Iroquois used the bounty of the forests, lakes, and rivers to meet many of their needs.
— The Iroquois made their homes, canoes, cookware, and many tools from wood.
— Men hunted deer, bears, and rabbits as a source of food and clothing.
— Women planted corn, beans, and squash—crops called the "*Three Sisters.*"
— Lakes provided fish and a means of transportation for the Iroquois.

People Of The Longhouse

Students may be surprised to learn that the Iroquois lived in homes similar to apartment buildings! Their homes, called *longhouses*, were made from the bark and wood of elm trees. Longhouses were built in many sizes, but the average home measured 25 x 80 feet. A longhouse was separated into several sections that each housed a family. Each section contained a cooking fire and raised platforms covered by reed mats or furs for sleeping or sitting.

Compare life in an Iroquois longhouse with life in a modern apartment building. After presenting students with pictures and information about longhouses, have each child create a Venn diagram, labeling one circle "Longhouse" and the other circle "My House." Ask students to fill each circle with characteristics that are unique to that type of house. Challenge students to fill the center of the Venn diagram with characteristics that the two types of houses have in common.

Allow students to share their Venn diagrams; then give each student a 12" x 18" sheet of white construction paper and crayons. Have a student fold her paper in half; then ask her to draw a longhouse on one half and her own house on the other half. Encourage the child to write a sentence under each house that tells why it would make a great home. Have students share their reasons.

Decorative Clothing

For a lesson on Iroquois clothing, read aloud from *The Iroquois* by Craig A. Doherty & Katherine M. Doherty (Franklin Watts, 1989). Students will learn that, in summer, Iroquois women wore buckskin skirts and leggings. Men wore breechcloths or kilts. In winter women wore dresses with leggings and moccasins. Men wore leggings, shirts, breechcloths, moccasins, and caps. Both wore furs in the winter to keep warm. In addition, the Iroquois dyed deer hides for clothing and decorated their garments with dyed moose hair and porcupine quills. After the Europeans arrived, the Iroquois began embroidering woven cloth with small glass beads. Women wore hair ornaments and beaded jewelry. At one time, extensive tattooing was common among Iroquois men.

To show the continuing influence of Native American dress, bring in examples of present-day clothing, footwear, or beaded jewelry that have native designs, or show adaptations of native clothing. Ask students to think of reasons why these items are in fashion today. (Perhaps the Iroquois style of dress was not only decorative but comfortable.) Provide students with craft beads to string on leather cords to create original bracelets or anklets. Allow students to wear their designs as reminders of the decorative style of the Iroquois.

Bark Baskets

The Iroquois used the bark of trees to make baskets. They often coated these baskets with pine pitch to make them waterproof. Explain that these lightweight, waterproof bark baskets were used for gathering wild berries, nuts, and water. Bigger baskets were used to gather corn, beans, and squash.

If possible invite a basket maker to demonstrate how a bark basket is made. After discussing the uses of these versatile baskets, fill some baskets with a favorite Native American treat—popcorn! Pass the baskets around your story circle as you tell the tale of Sky Woman below.

Turtle-Shell Rattles

Share this Iroquois tale of the turtle and then have students create turtle-shell rattles for a music lesson. Iroquois legend has it that the earth was once covered with water. One day Sky Woman fell from the Sky World and plummeted toward the water. Swans caught Sky Woman and placed her on the back of a giant sea turtle. Other animals began to heap mud upon the sea turtle's back to make a land on which Sky Woman could live. Sky Woman planted seeds so the earth would have plants. Thus the earth was formed for Sky Woman and her children and her children's children.

After sharing this legend, invite each child to celebrate the turtle's gift of land by making turtle-shell rattles. Each student will need two disposable plastic bowls, a tongue depressor, tempera paint, a paintbrush, dried beans or popcorn kernels, and masking tape. To make a rattle, a student places a handful of dried beans or popcorn kernels into a bowl. He places the second bowl onto the first bowl in an inverted position as shown. The child slides the tongue depressor between the bowls to make a handle. Help each child seal his bowls together with masking tape, securing the handle with tape as well. The child paints the bowls to resemble the shell of a turtle. Students will enjoy using their rattles to make rhythmic patterns for their classmates to replicate.

Trading Wampum

Engage students in making wampum to improve their patterning skills. Tell students that the Iroquois treasured wampum, which were belts or strips of beads made from white and purple seashells. Wampum beads were strung in a variety of patterns. Designs commemorated important events, symbolized treaties, and identified messengers. Wampum was traded for goods, and it was given as gifts at important council meetings. If possible, show students an actual wampum strip or a picture of one; then invite each child to create a wampum belt of her own. Reproduce a class supply of the wampum grid on page 59. Give each student one wampum grid, one purple crayon, and one white crayon.

Divide your class into groups of three students each. Have each child use her crayons to color the squares in the first section of her wampum grid. Ask each group member to trade wampum grids within the group; then have each child copy her classmate's design on the second section of the grid. Have students continue trading grids until the wampum belt is complete. If desired a child can punch a hole in each end of her belt, run a length of yarn through each hole, and tie the colorful wampum belt around her waist.

Iroquois Thanksgiving

Explain to students that the Iroquois were good farmers who relied on a bountiful harvest of corn, beans, and squash to get them through the hard winters. The Green Corn Festival was the autumn celebration to give thanks for the harvest of the three crops known as the *"Three Sisters."* They also grew pumpkins and some tobacco for ceremonial purposes.

In the early spring, the Iroquois celebrated the rising of the sap with a Maple Dance. After boring holes in maple trees, the Iroquois collected the sweet maple sap and boiled it to make maple syrup and sugar. The Iroquois danced to give thanks to the maple trees and to the Creator who had made the maple trees. Later the Iroquois held an annual Strawberry Festival to thank the strawberry spirit and the Creator for the first ripe strawberries.

To conclude your unit on the Iroquois, plan a festival of Iroquois foods. Create a display of the foods the Iroquois gathered. Place fresh corn, squash, pumpkins, apples, strawberries, dried kidney beans, and walnuts in the shell in individual baskets on a table. Discuss how each food grows and is gathered. Have parents prepare a version of Iroquois corn soup for tasting. Wrap up your Iroquois festival with a treat of maple-sugar candy as you read aloud *Little Runner Of The Longhouse* by Betty Baker (Harper & Row Publishers, Inc.; 1962).

Books About The Iroquois

Indians Of The Eastern Woodlands by Sally Sheppard (Franklin Watts, Inc.; 1975)
The Iroquois: People Of The Northeast by Evelyn Wolfson (The Millbrook Press, 1992)
The Iroquois Indians by Victoria Sherrow (Chelsea House Publishers, 1992)
The Naked Bear: Folktales Of The Iroquois by John Bierhorst (William Morrow & Company, 1987)

Wampum Belt

The Iroquois strung white and purple beads to make wampum strips or belts. The beads were made from seashells. The wampum was traded for food, furs, or tools. Wampum belts were given as gifts. The pattern on the belt was a symbol of an important event such as the signing of a peace treaty.

Follow these directions to make your own wampum belt.
1. Color in a pattern on Grid A. Use a purple crayon.
2. Have a friend repeat your pattern on Grid B.
3. Ask another friend to repeat the pattern on Grid C.
4. Cut out your wampum strip on the dotted lines.
5. Fold a strip of construction paper.
6. Glue your strip to the construction paper.
7. Punch a hole at each end.
8. String yarn through the holes and tie.

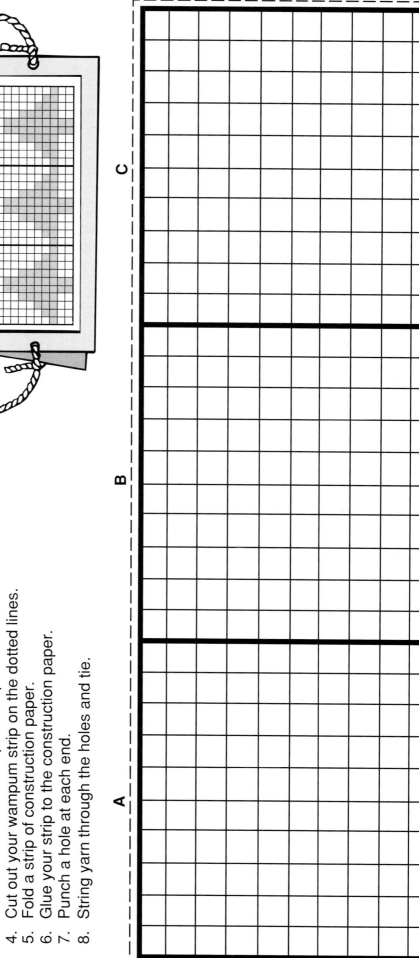

The Sioux

The free-spirited Sioux, the horsemen of the plains, are the natives associated most often with the American Wild West. Unfortunately, the savage Indian portrayed in face paint and warbonnet became a stereotype for all Native Americans. Students need to learn that this image is incorrect. Indeed, the Sioux rode horses and hunted buffalo, and adult men wore feathered headdresses for ceremonial purposes. But emphasize that, as with other natives, the environment—not war—shaped the daily lives of the Sioux tribes.

Ideas by Resa Audet and Kathy Wolf

The People Of The Plains

To introduce the study of the Sioux, share the story of *The Girl Who Loved Wild Horses* by Paul Goble (Scholastic Inc., 1978). Discuss why horses were so important to the Sioux. Then point out the flora and fauna of the Plains, so richly illustrated by the artist. Challenge older students to identify as many of the plants and animals as they can. Make a class list of plants and animals of the Plains. Have each child color the North American Plains area on a map; then share these facts with students:

—The Sioux are a group of tribes who speak a similar language and lived in the Plains regions of Nebraska, Wyoming, Minnesota, Montana, and the Dakotas.

—Many Sioux tribes once depended on the buffalo for their food, clothing, shelter, and tools. These tribes moved often to follow migrating herds of buffalo.

—Most Sioux men were hunters and warriors.

—Sioux women were responsible for cooking, making clothing and tepees, taking care of the children, and packing and carrying the tribe's belongings.

—The Sioux traveled on horseback and on foot. They carried their belongings on *travois,* stretcherlike carriers made by securing buffalo hides between poles.

Tortilla Tepees

The Sioux lived in tentlike homes called *tepees.* Explain that tepees were perfect homes for the nomadic Sioux, who moved frequently to follow the buffalo herds. Tepees were made from buffalo hides, which were plentiful on the Plains. Tepees were portable and could be quickly erected by the women. Have students imagine living every day in tents with their families.

Show students a picture of a tepee or Sioux encampment; then help them create a model Sioux village. Each child will need one half of a flour tortilla, markers, and tape. Have each child lay the tortilla flat; then have him use markers to decorate it with Native American symbols. Help each child fold the tortilla into a cone shape; then have him tape the top of the tortilla in place. Have the child carefully tear off a section at the bottom to create a doorway as shown. Allow the tortillas to dry; then remove the tape. Handle with care as the tepees will be fragile. Display the tepees on a large table. Invite students to create a camp scene by designing props—such as people, cooking fires, horses, and herds of buffalo—using construction paper, clay, and other craft materials.

idea submitted by Nancy Matthews

Parfleche Storage

How did the nomadic Sioux people store and carry their food? They used *parfleches*. A parfleche was a buffalo-hide pouch that was used for storing clothing or foods such as jerky and *pemmican*—a dried mixture of fat and meat. The Sioux usually decorated their parfleches with paint. Parfleches were considered to be valuable gifts.

Help each student make a parfleche of his own to carry a snack of beef jerky. Each student will need a copy of the pattern on page 64, a piece of brown or tan felt, fabric paints, yarn, a black marker, scissors, and a hole puncher. Instruct each student to follow the steps below to assemble a parfleche.

Directions For Making Parfleches

1. Cut out and punch holes in the pattern.
2. Trace the pattern, including the holes, onto the felt using a black marker.
3. Cut out and punch holes in the felt pattern.
4. Thread a six-inch length of yarn through each of the two holes on the left side of the felt pattern; then thread a six-inch length of yarn through the top hole as shown.
5. Use fabric paint to create designs on the outside of the parfleche.
6. Provide each student with a strip of beef jerky wrapped in paper.
7. To close the parfleche, follow the steps at right.

Encourage each student to take his parfleche home to share the snack and some fascinating facts that he has learned about the Sioux.

Winter Counts

Introduce students to the Sioux calendar known as the Winter Count. Explain that the Sioux counted the years by the passing of winters. To record historical events that occurred in a given year, a tribe painted symbolic pictures of the event on a large piece of animal hide. The first picture was placed in the center of the hide; then the pictures for subsequent years were arranged in a spiral shape around the center. Show students a picture of a Winter Count. Then let students create their own Winter Counts to record memories!

Have each child cut a brown, paper grocery bag in the shape of an animal hide. Instruct her to repeatedly crumple the paper to make it soft. After laying the paper flat, have each child draw or paint several pictures that illustrate important events or experiences in her life. Remind her to draw the earliest event in the center of the hide and to arrange additional pictures in a spiral shape as shown. Encourage each child to share her Winter Count with the class; then have her take her Winter Count home to share with her family.

Musical Impressions

Surround students with the sounds of Native American music. Explain that music was an integral part of life for the Sioux. Drums, flutes, and the human voice were used to make music for many occasions. There were lullabies, love songs, and songs for ceremonies, games, powwows, and funerals. Music was also a form of communication. Certain tunes played on a flute, for example, could relay messages from the player to the listener.

Play an audiotape of Lakota Sioux music (see suggestions below). Discuss with students the feelings that the music evokes. Ask, "Does the music make you feel sadness or joy? Is the tone solemn or lighthearted?" If possible, read some Native American poetry and have students pair poetry with the music. *Dancing Teepees: Poems Of American Indian Youth* selected by Virginia Driving Hawk Sneve (Holiday House, Inc.; 1989) is a good source. Or read Carl Sandburg's poem "Buffalo Dusk," found in *Sing A Song Of Popcorn* (Scholastic Inc., 1988). Your students will learn to appreciate the sounds of Native American music with their hearts as well as their ears.

- *Dream Catcher* by Tokeya Inajin (Kevin Locke). Available from Music For Little People at 1-800-727-2233 (cassette, #2696 @ $9.98; or CD, #D2696 @ $12.98).
- *Keepers Of The Dream* by Tokeya Inajin (Kevin Locke). Available from Music For Little People at 1-800-727-2233 (cassette, #2968 @ $9.98; or CD, #D2968 @ $13.98).

Sign Talk

Teach students to communicate silently with Native American sign language. Explain that there were many different tribes living on the Plains long ago. Many of them did not speak the same language. In order to foster better communication among the tribes, the Sioux and some of their neighbors developed a regional sign language based on gestures. Sign language was used within a tribe as well. Elderly people with poor hearing used sign language. Men sign-talked while hunting so they would not spook the buffalo. Even early European settlers learned to communicate with Native Americans by using sign language.

To teach students how to sign-talk, share *North American Indian Sign Language* by Karen Liptak (Scholastic Inc., 1990). Divide your class into student groups. Have each group choose and practice one of the examples illustrated in the book. Encourage students to combine the words to create messages to each other if silence is necessary and sign language is teacher-approved.

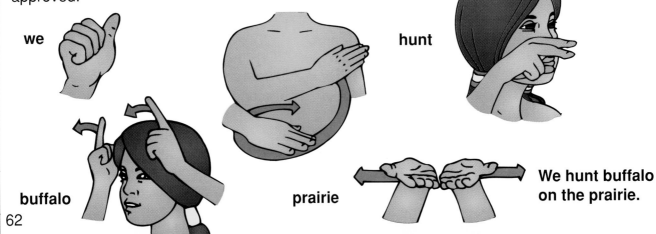

we

hunt

buffalo

prairie

We hunt buffalo on the prairie.

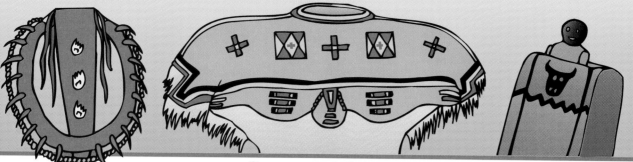

Ceremonial Drums

Students can participate in a celebration of Native American music and dance by making and playing ceremonial drums. Collect and distribute various size containers with lids (Pringles® cans, oatmeal canisters, large and small tin cans, etc.). Provide students with construction paper, glue, scissors, markers, two unsharpened pencils, and two rubber bands. Have each student cut the paper to fit his drum, then decorate it with the markers. Instruct each student to wrap the construction paper around his container and glue it in place. To make drumsticks, wrap a rubber band around the eraser end of one of the pencils to make a knoblike end. Repeat the process for the other pencil. Students can place their drums between their knees or on a flat surface and beat out a rhythm.

Helpful Horses

Horses were highly valued by the Sioux people. They were used to carry tepees and other belongings from one campsite to another. Horses made travelling easier, and they made buffalo hunting safer and more productive. A family was considered wealthy if it owned many ponies. After discussing the importance of horses to the Sioux, read *The Mud Pony* retold by Caron Lee Cohen (Scholastic Inc., 1989). In this traditional tale from the Plains Indians, a young boy makes a pony from mud. After the boy is accidentally abandoned by his tribe, the mud pony comes to life and returns the boy to his people.

After reading this story, let your youngsters make clay horses of their own. Provide pictures of many different kinds of horses. Have each student make a horse using baker's clay (see the recipe below). Allow the clay to dry; then have each student paint his horse using tempera paints. Ask each child to name his horse; then have him write a story featuring his clay companion.

Baker's Clay
(for approximately 8 students)
2 cups flour
1 cup salt
3/4 cup water

Mix all the ingredients together.
Add additional water, if necessary.
Knead until smooth.

More Books About The Sioux

The Moon Of Falling Leaves by Cary B. Ziter (Franklin Watts, 1988)
The Sioux by Elaine Landau (Franklin Watts, 1989)
The Teton Sioux: People Of The Plains by Evelyn Wolfson (The Millbrook Press, 1992)
Buffalo Dance: A Blackfoot Legend retold by Nancy Van Laan (Little, Brown and Company; 1993)

Pattern

Use with "Parfleche Storage" on page 61.

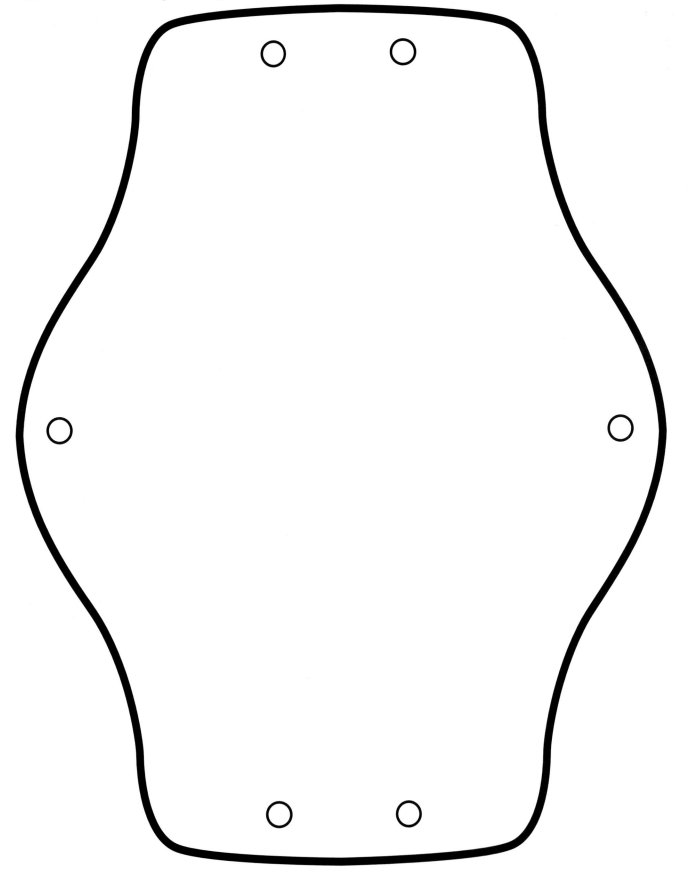

The Navajo

by Kathy Wolf

The Navajo call themselves *Dinéh,* The People. Over a thousand years ago, their ancestors migrated to the Southwest from Alaska and Canada. Their neighbors, the Pueblos, taught them to grow corn and to weave. The Spanish introduced sheep into the area, prompting the Navajo to raise large herds of sheep for wool and meat. Navajo craftsmen also learned silversmithing from the Spanish.

The Navajo have successfully borrowed techniques from other cultures and adapted to life in their arid land. Today they are the largest group of Native Americans in the United States, with tribal wealth from oil and coal.

Print the following facts on a class chart; then share them with your students. Locate the Navajo reservation, the largest in the nation, on a map of the United States.

— The Navajo live in the *Four Corners* area of the United States where New Mexico, Arizona, Colorado, and Utah come together.
— Some Navajo live in traditional individual homes called *hogans* made of earth and wooden poles or logs. Navajo who live in modern homes may still have hogans for religious purposes.
— Today many Navajo raise herds of cattle, sheep, or goats. Others work in the mines and oil fields of the Southwest, or as teachers and engineers.
— The Navajo are known for their beautiful crafts that include masterfully woven woolen blankets and fine jewelry of turquoise and silver.
— Sandpaintings are created for healing ceremonies by a Navajo healer or shaman called *Hatali.* These designs—painted with colored earth, pollen, and cornmeal—serve as altars upon which ailing individuals sit or lie during rituals.

To introduce new vocabulary to students, duplicate the sheep pattern on page 72 and label each of 20 sheep cutouts with a word: *arid, canyon, carding, coyote, desert, flock, hogan, loom, mesa, reservation, sandpainting, shaman, shearing, sheepherder, silversmith, Spanish, spindle, tumbleweed, turquoise, weave.* Have students place the sheep in alphabetical order and pin them to a bulletin board to create a border.

A Hogan Is A Home

The Navajo were once nomadic herders engaged in gathering, hunting, and some farming. They live in simple homes called *hogans* near their flocks and fields. The hogan is an octagonal, windowless, one-room, domed shelter made of earth and logs. The mud between the timbers keeps it cool in summer and cozy in winter. Legend has it that the first hogan was built by the Holy People with the doorway facing east. Thus, hogan doorways always face east. Inside a hogan, bedding is piled against the walls and a stove stands in the center. An extended family may live in one room without electricity or plumbing.

Help students compare living in an isolated hogan on a reservation to how they live. Have students discuss why Navajo people may prefer to live on a reservation rather than in any other community. Ask students to think of reasons why Navajo children learn English as well as their own Navajo language.

Explain that a larger Navajo community today may have a supermarket, a burger restaurant, a motel, and a pizza place. Navajo children watch TV, eat fast food, play basketball, and roller-skate like many Americans. To complete the lesson, have students create a mural showing a collage of Navajo life. For inspiration share the wonderful paintings of Shonto Begay found in *Navajo: Visions And Voices Across The Mesa* (Scholastic Inc., 1995).

Coyote The Trickster

The Navajo tell their children stories of long ago that explain the creation of the earth, the elements of nature, and reasons why—why Navajo girls learn to weave or why one must sprinkle corn pollen if a coyote crosses one's path. Coyote is a character that often appears in legends of the Southwest Indians. This wily animal is portrayed as a conniving trickster, a braggart, and an inquisitive troublemaker. In many ways, Coyote is thoroughly human!

To introduce students to the southwestern tradition of coyote legends, read aloud *Coyote: A Trickster Tale From The American Southwest* by Gerald McDermott (Harcourt Brace & Company, 1994) based on the Zuni folktale. After reading, ask students to think what lesson can be learned from this tale. Discuss how the coyote's vanity caused him to be a bore and left him forever with a burnt, black-tipped tail.

Read other coyote stories such as *Coyote Places The Stars* by Harriet Peck Taylor (Bradbury Press, 1993) and *Coyote And The Magic Words* by Phyllis Root (Lothrop, Lee & Shepard Books; 1993). Discuss how Coyote is similar or different in each story. Then have each student write and illustrate another adventure for crafty Coyote. Share these tales in a circle at storytime.

Student Silversmiths

Navajo silversmiths are known for their intricate silver and turquoise jewelry. Share examples (or pictures) of jewelry made by Navajo craftsmen, such as a concha belt or a squash-blossom necklace with its bell-shaped pendants. If possible, invite a jewelry maker to demonstrate how he works with silver and precious stones to create Native American designs. Then give students the opportunity to become silversmiths and design their own concha belts or pendants.

For making a "silver" concha, provide each student with a three-inch circular disk cut from cardboard or poster board. Cut diamond shapes in the center of each disk, as shown, with an X-acto® knife. Have each student cover his disk with a five-inch square of aluminum foil; then tape the foil in place. Have him use a pencil to poke the foil through the diamond-shaped slits from the front; then have him use the pencil to lightly draw a design on the foil and to punch in the design with the pencil point. Demonstrate how to apply turquoise paint or glue turquoise beads to simulate precious stones.

When the designs are dry, provide the boys with three-inch-wide strips of fabric with which to make belts. Have each boy poke the fabric strip through the center slits from the back and center the concha on his belt. Give each girl a 12-inch length of cord to thread through the slits in the ornament and tie to make a necklace. When the projects have been completed, each student will have a remembrance of splendid Navajo silversmithing to wear.

Weaving Tales

Weaving is more than a craft or hobby to the Navajo. Some Navajo rugs and blankets are prized works of art that are displayed in museums. Although the money from the sale of rugs and blankets is an essential part of many family incomes, each woven piece is also like a history of the people. Different Navajo areas are known for their distinct colors, designs, and patterns. In a return to the past, Navajo rugs are being woven with unique homespun yarns rather than commercial yarns and are valued for the stories they tell. When Navajo girls learn to weave, they are told the stories and legends of their people. The tales are woven into the process of making a rug so they are handed down from generation to generation.

To introduce students to how a Navajo rug is made, read *Songs From The Loom: A Navajo Girl Learns to Weave* by Monty Roessel (Lerner Publications Company, 1995). The step-by-step photographs show how a modern-day Navajo girl and her grandmother shear sheep, card the wool, and then spin it. Together they gather plants to dye wool. As the girl creates her own rug, she learns respect for the loom and the tools she uses. Ask students to tell how they can apply this lesson to the care of their own possessions. Together, sequence the steps for making the rug. List them on a class chart. If possible, display a Navajo rug and have a weaver demonstrate the steps followed to make the rug.

After reading the tale in the aforementioned book of how Spider Woman teaches Changing Woman to weave, have students think of reasons why the Navajo tell these stories. Discuss what might happen if parents and grandparents do not tell the old stories to Navajo children.

For creative writing, ask each student to weave another tale. Ask the student to imagine where Spider Woman got the colors for her new rug or to tell what happened when Changing Woman discovered a loom in the sky. Have students illustrate their stories. To decorate their papers, have students weave lengths of yarn into their illustrations. Bind the tales in a notebook or display them on a bulletin board titled "Tales From The Loom."

More Books About The Navajo

Annie And The Old One by Miska Miles (Little, Brown, And Company; 1971)
Katie Henio: Navajo Sheepherder by Peggy Thomson (Cobblehill Books, 1995)
Turquoise Boy: A Navajo Legend written and adapted by Terri Cohlene (Watermill Press, 1990)
The Goat In The Rug by Geraldine as told to Charles L. Blood and Martin Link (Four Winds Press, 1993)

The Tlingits

The Land Of Wood And Water

Prior to your study of the Tlingits, use a large wall map to show students the areas that Native Americans of the Pacific Northwest inhabited. If possible, locate pictures of the Pacific Northwest coast to show to students. Prepare to guide them to the understanding that wood and water influenced the lives of the Native Americans who lived in this area.

Then locate a copy of the book *Indians Of The Pacific Northwest* by Karen Liptak (The First Americans series: Facts On File, Inc.; 1991). Share pictures and excerpts from the book with students. Then explain that you'll be studying the Tlingits, a group of Native Americans who lived in the Pacific Northwest. Share the following background information with your students:

— The Tlingits lived in what is now southeastern Alaska.
— The Tlingits lived in homes made of cedar planks. Each home had an inside framework and an outer covering that could either be moved from location to location or destroyed. Many people lived in one house.
— The Tlingits hunted for bear, deer, and seals; fished for salmon and halibut; and gathered berries and shellfish, such as oysters and clams.
— The Tlingits built large, oceangoing canoes from hollowed-out cedar logs.
— Cedar bark provided the Tlingits with material for their clothing.

Chilkat Robes

Tell students that the Chilkat—a division of the Tlingit—were expert robe makers. The robes, which were made of dog or mountain-goat wool and cedar bark, were used as shawls and dancing costumes and were worn on ceremonial occasions. Sometimes the robes were traded for dentalia snails, shells, or slaves.

Then use a teacher resource such as *Indians Of The Northwest Coast* by Peter R. Gerber (Facts On File Publications, 1989) to locate pictures of Native Americans in ceremonial costume. Next let each student create his own robe similar to the one shown. To make a robe, each student will need to cut out the side panels of a large grocery bag so that it will lay flat. Then have each student use tempera paint and paintbrushes, crayons, or markers to decorate his robe. After his project has dried, have the student hole-punch a series of equally spaced holes along the sides and bottom of his robe. Supply each student with five-inch lengths of white yarn and have him loop a yarn length through each hole as shown to make a fringe for his robe. Allow students to model their robes for another class.

The Salmon Story

Remind students that salmon was very important to the Tlingits. Not only was salmon eaten fresh and dried, the eggs were eaten too. Since salmon was so important, a tribe might know 200 different ways to prepare the fish. None of the salmon was wasted either. The skins were used to make clothing, boots, and waterproof linings for baskets.

Use the book *Swimmer* by Shelley Gill (Paws IV Publishing, 1995) to help students learn more about the life cycle of this fascinating fish. Discuss the story; then let students sample a small chunk of salmon that has been placed atop a cracker.

The Stick Game

Tell students that one very popular game played by the Tlingits was the stick game. The game was played with a bundle of sticks that were each decorated at one end with a carving or a painting. To play, a player divided the sticks into two bundles and held one bundle in each hand. The player would then ask his opponent to guess which bundle contained a particular stick or whether a bundle had an even or odd number of sticks in it.

Then give your students the opportunity to play the stick game. Place 91 wooden craft sticks that have each been labeled with a number between 10 and 100 into a pouch. (A pouch can be made by folding a piece of 9" x 12" brown construction paper in half and stapling the sides.) Put the pouch at a center and let pairs of students visit the center to play the game as described.

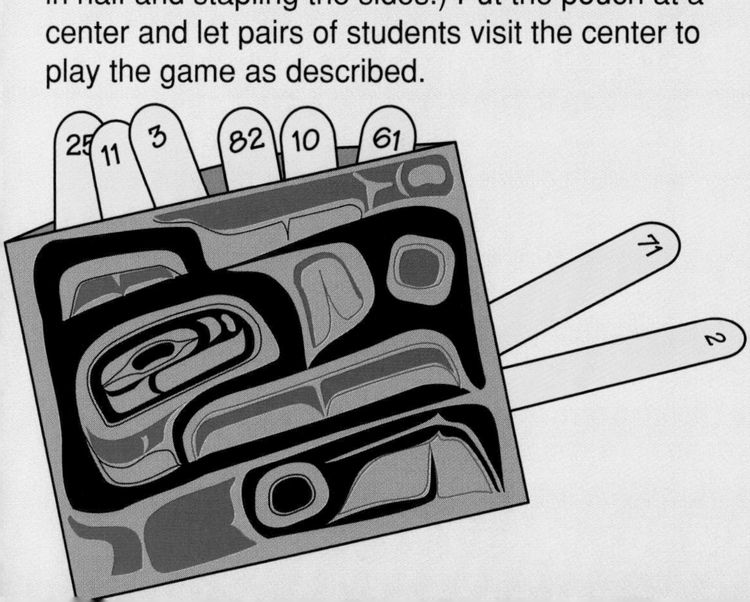

Trickster Tales

Explain to students that among the Tlingits, Raven was an important character in stories and tales. The Tlingits believed that Raven—who was considered a trickster, mischief maker, and hero—created the world and often did good deeds. Afterward share a Raven story like *Raven: A Trickster Tale From The Pacific Northwest* by Gerald McDermott (Scholastic Inc., 1993) or "Raven, The River Maker" included in the book *In A Circle Long Ago: A Treasury Of Native Lore From North America* by Nancy Van Laan (Apple Soup Books, 1995).

Then have each student write her own Raven story. Begin by brainstorming topics for Raven tales with students and listing them on the board. Allow each student to select a topic of her choice, then write a story. Ask volunteers to share their stories with classmates; then bind the stories in a classroom collection called "Our Trickster Tales." For a fun variation, allow students to act out their trickster tales (see "Marvelous Masks" below).

Marvelous Masks

Tell students that masks were considered by the Tlingits (and other Native Americans of the Pacific Northwest) to be very valuable possessions. Very elaborate and intricate in design, masks were worn for ceremonies, rituals, healing the sick, and for fun.

Then let each student make his own raven mask that can be worn for fun or while acting out his trickster tale. To make a raven mask, give each student one-half of a nine-inch paper plate that has been cut as shown. Have each student use a circle template to trace two eyes on his mask, then cut them out. Working atop a sheet of newspaper, have each student sponge-paint his paper plate black. Next give each child a copy of the beak pattern on page 72. Tell the student to color and cut out the beak, then fold on the dotted lines and glue the beak where indicated. Have each student glue his beak on his mask as shown. Then staple a length of elastic to each student's mask to make it suitable for wearing. If desired, invite students to make other paper-plate masks to assist them in acting out their trickster tales.

How Raven Made
The Water Flow

How Raven Made
The Flowers Bloom

How Raven Made
Night And Day

Tlingit Totem Poles

Explain to students that one of the trademarks of the Native Americans of the Pacific Northwest were their totem poles. The Tlingits—one of the many groups who carved these spectacular symbols of the Northwest—used totem poles to record legends or honor important people. Tell students that only well-to-do and respected men were allowed to own totem poles. When a totem pole was needed, a carver was asked to do the job. The carver, who was well paid for his services, could become very wealthy. Often it took a year or more to complete a pole; then the carver was paid. Items used for payment could include food, blankets, and other valuables. Share the book *Totem Pole* by Diane Hoyt-Goldsmith (Scholastic Inc., 1990) with your students. This well-illustrated resource follows the work of a Tsimshian carver as he creates a totem pole.

Afterward, divide students into groups of five and allow each group to make a totem pole. To do that, each student in each group will need to bring an empty, 26-ounce salt container from home. Give each student a 5 1/2" x 12" piece of wood-grain Con-Tact® paper. Without peeling away the backing, instruct the student to wrap the paper around his salt container and secure it in place with pieces of adhesive tape. Then, working with the taped seam in the back, have each child glue pieces of construction paper to the container to create an animal face. Other facial details may be added with permanent markers. After the members of one group have finished decorating their containers, align the seams in the back and glue the containers one atop the other to form a totem pole. Repeat this process for each remaining group. Plan to hold a potlatch (see "A Perfect Potlatch" on page 72) to celebrate the raising of your classroom totem poles.

Idea submitted by Susan D. Meyer

A Perfect Potlatch

Tell students that Tlingit clans held special ceremonies—called *pot-latches*—that allowed them to demonstrate their status and wealth to their guests. A potlatch marked an important event like a marriage, a special birth, a move to a new dwelling, or the raising of a new totem pole. These celebrations could sometimes last for days. During potlatches, guests were fed, housed, and presented with gifts such as canoes, sealskins, barrels of whale oil, and slaves. Although this may sound foreign to us, to the Tlingits it was considered an honor to give away one's wealth. After the potlatch had ended, the guests were obligated to reciprocate. They had to hold their own pot-latches and in return present their guests with gifts that were more valuable than the ones they received.

Afterward ask students if they think it's common nowadays for people to give away their precious belongings. Survey students to find out how many of them would be willing to give away a treasured toy—even if they would receive some-thing in return. Then plan to hold a potlatch in honor of the completion of your classroom totem poles. To prepare for the potlatch, give each student a maga-zine or catalog and an index card. From the magazine, have each student cut out one item that he feels would be suitable to give as a gift, then glue it to the index card. Next divide students into two groups. Have the groups sit down facing each other; then designate one group as the host of the potlatch. In turn, have each member of the host group present a member of the guest group with a gift. Then ask each member of the guest group to present a member of the host group with a gift. Remind members of the guest group that their gifts should be more valuable than the gifts that they were presented with.

Beak Pattern
Use with "Marvelous Masks" on page 70.

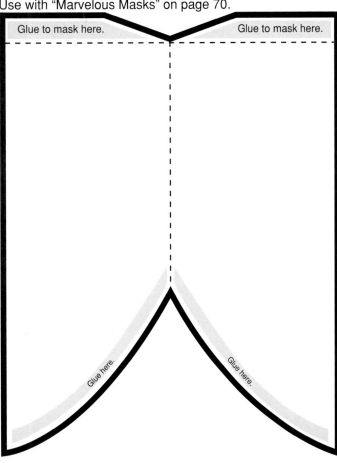

Glue to mask here.　　Glue to mask here.

Glue here.　　Glue here.

Sheep Pattern
Use with "The Navajo" on page 65.

Name _____

Native American Cultural Areas

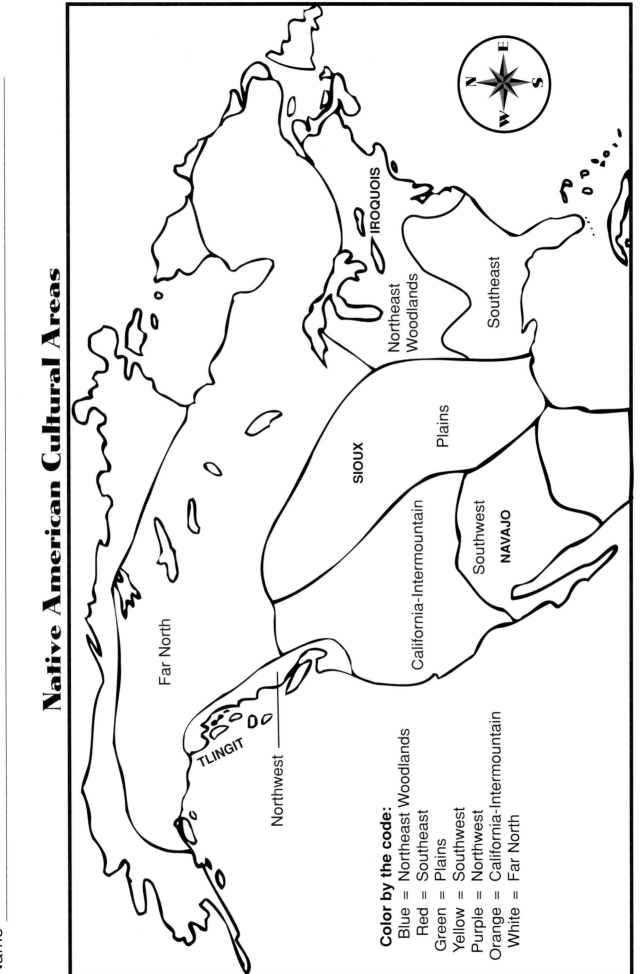

Far North

TLINGIT

Northwest

SIOUX

Plains

California-Intermountain

Southwest

NAVAJO

Northeast
Woodlands

IROQUOIS

Southeast

Color by the code:
Blue = Northeast Woodlands
Red = Southeast
Green = Plains
Yellow = Southwest
Purple = Northwest
Orange = California-Intermountain
White = Far North

Colonial America

Help your students discover how different life was for boys and girls in colonial America. Then follow up with a unit on westward expansion and pioneer life.

Ideas by Carmel F. White

Log Cabin Life

Provide illustrations of log cabins and colonial clapboard houses; then help students deduce that the most common building material during the colonial period was wood. Some settlers chose to build homes of logs, while others cut the logs into thick boards. Both sealed the spaces between each piece of wood with cement made of clay or mud.

Create log cabins for your bulletin board using puffy paint. To make puffy paint, mix equal parts of flour and salt in a large bowl. Add enough water to make a mixture the consistency of icing. Add brown, powdered tempera paint to get a wood color. The mixture will be fairly thick. Pour the puffy paint into plastic squeeze bottles—the kind used for ketchup or mustard works well. Cut off enough of the tip of the squeeze bottle to create an opening that will allow the paint to squeeze out in a thick line. Make some gray puffy paint to use as cement and for creating stone chimneys. Squeeze this gray paint through a squeeze bottle with a tip that has a smaller opening. If the puffy paint is too thick to squeeze easily, add water a small amount at a time to thin it.

Have students squeeze the puffy paint onto cardboard or heavy paper that you have cut into log-cabin shapes as shown. The puffy paint will dry in puffy shapes. To give each log cabin a realistic-looking thatched roof, have the student glue on dried parsley or another green herb. Allow the projects to dry overnight; then display them on your bulletin board with construction-paper trees and the title "Log Cabins In The Woods."

Hearthside Reading

Family life in colonial times centered around the hearth. Here the family found warmth, food, and family togetherness. Construct a large classroom fireplace from an appliance box and let this hearth be your class gathering place throughout your study of colonial times. An easy way to achieve the look of stone is to paint the box with a light gray paint, cut large stone shapes from sponges, and sponge-paint dark gray stones on top of the dry light gray paint. Children can help you paint the fireplace. The top of the box can serve as a mantle where you may want to display candles or dried flowers. Add a few logs and a crepe-paper fire, and gather your colonial family around the hearth for some family time.

Hornbook Journals

Most colonial children were taught at home. Some children, ages six to eight, might have attended a *dame school*. A dame schoolteacher held class in her home. Children came to learn the alphabet, some reading, and *ciphering* (simple arithmetic). Very few people could write. Many lessons involved memorizing rhymes. Hornbooks were often the only texts. A hornbook was a wooden paddle to which a page of writing had been attached. For durability, the page was covered with a thin sheet of horn; thus the name *hornbook.*

To make hornbook journals for creative writing, fold one sheet of 9" x 12" brown construction paper in half. Trace the hornbook pattern on page 77 on the construction paper, being careful to line up the pattern with the fold of the construction paper. Cut out the hornbook, but do not cut on the fold. Cut a piece of white paper using the smaller inside pattern and write the title as shown. Glue this white paper to the front of the hornbook cutout. Staple several sheets of 5 1/2" square paper inside the horn book.

For this lesson ask students to pretend they are in a one-room schoolhouse. Have each child take out his hornbook and write about or draw pictures of one of these suggested topics: "My Favorite Rhyme," "Colonial School Days," "My Log-Cabin Home," or "My Favorite Colonial Toy."

Journey Cake, Ho!

Read Ruth Sawyer's *Journey Cake, Ho!* (The Viking Press, 1982) to introduce students to a common food of colonial times. Pancakes made of cornmeal and buttermilk, then baked or fried on a hot griddle, were often carried on long journeys and thus came to be called *journey cakes.*

After reading *Journey Cake, Ho!*, your young settlers will enjoy making and tasting journey cakes. Invite some parents to visit the classroom and help in the preparation of the journey cakes.

Journey Cakes

1 cup yellow cornmeal	1/4 teaspoon baking soda
1/4 cup flour	1 teaspoon salt
1 cup boiling water	2 tablespoons butter, melted
1 cup buttermilk	1 egg, lightly beaten

Combine the cornmeal and salt. Slowly stir in the boiling water and melted butter. Cover and let stand for ten minutes. Stir in the buttermilk and egg. Combine the flour and baking soda, and stir quickly into the batter. This batter is very thin. Spoon a tablespoon of batter at a time onto a medium -hot griddle that has been sprayed with a vegetable spray. (An electric frying pan works well, too.) Turn only once. Stir batter often and keep the griddle well sprayed. Serve with maple syrup. Makes about 40 small pancakes.

Cornhusk Dolls

Although boys and girls were kept busy with chores such as gathering wood and water, gardening, weaving, sewing, and making candles and soap, they did find time for some fun and games. Many girls enjoyed making and playing with dolls. Of course, they used materials that were readily available in their homes. One such doll was made of cornhusks.

To make cornhusk dolls, trace the doll-frame pattern below on cardboard and cut out one for each child. Give each child nine pieces of cornhusk (available in craft stores), a paper towel, and a cardboard doll pattern. Pass around a plant mister that you have filled with water and have each child lightly mist both sides of each cornhusk. Have students place the moist cornhusks on their paper towels. (The cornhusks need to moisten for at least three minutes so that you can bend them without breaking them.)

Next gently pat the shucks dry. Take one husk and loop it from front to back over the top of the doll frame. Glue it in place with tacky glue (white glue will not work). Now make loops for the arms and glue them into place. Have the children examine the cornhusks, noting that one end is straight and the other end is pointed. Glue the straight ends of the cornhusks to the waist of the doll, allowing the points to form the doll's skirt. Add a bit of Spanish moss for hair and embellish the doll with ribbon scraps. Draw a face using permanent markers. These dolls make a lovely bulletin-board border.

Doll
Pattern

Cut one from folded brown construction paper.
Cut inside from white paper.

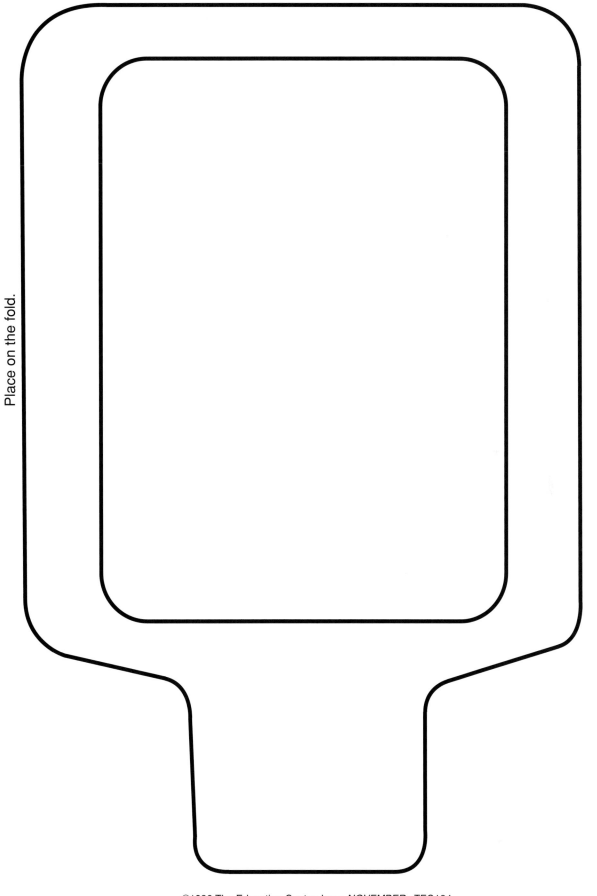

Place on the fold.

PIONEER LIFE
HEADIN' WEST

In the mid-1800s, covered wagons crossed our country by the thousands, carrying pioneer families west to new lands filled with promise. These rugged frontier families traveled many dangerous miles across vast plains, treacherous mountain ranges, wild forested areas, and seemingly endless deserts to reach fertile farmlands or stake claims to natural resources. Head up a classroom wagon train and lead your students along this trail of cross-curricular activities.

ideas by Kerry S. Ireland-Miller and Kathy Wolf

Westward, Ho!

Traveling in small covered wagons that could hold only the bare necessities, these adventurous families had hard choices to make. Before starting out, a lot of planning had to be done. Each family had to decide what trail to take to reach its intended destination, what animals were needed to pull its wagon, when to begin the journey to ensure the best weather, and whom to choose as a guide or trail master. Then pioneers had to decide which things to take and which things to leave behind. Anything not taken on the long and dangerous journey was sold or abandoned. Possessions littered the trails west as the pioneers had to decide again and again what they must relinquish to lighten the wagons on perilous crossings or difficult treks up mountains.

Your students will better understand these difficult decisions after you read aloud *The Josefina Story Quilt* by Eleanor Coerr (HarperCollins Publishers, 1986.) After reading, have student volunteers share their moving-day experiences. Compare their stories to how Faith and her family planned to move; then divide your class into small teams or "families." Explain to them that they are about to head west with the next wagon train from Independence, Missouri, and they need to decide what items they will bring with them on their long journey to California. Lead a discussion concerning the difference between a necessity and a luxury. Each team should develop a list of items, circling those that are needed for survival.

Circle The Wagons!

Share *If You Traveled West In A Covered Wagon* by Ellen Levine (Scholastic Inc., 1986); then circle the wagons to create a pioneer bulletin board! Help each team formed in the "Westward, Ho!" activity enlarge, color, and cut out the covered wagon pattern on page 81 on butcher paper. Mount the wagons in a circle on a bulletin board or line them up above the board in train formation. Have teams draw, label, and cut out the items they have chosen to bring along in their covered wagons. Have each team mount the pictures along with its list from "Westward, Ho!" on its wagon. Add the title and a border of student-made cactus cutouts. Have team members explain to the class the reasons behind their choices.

78

Fix Some Frontier Foods

Your students will feel like they're sitting in Ma and Pa Ingalls's cozy, little house on the prairie as they sample homemade dried apples, bird's nest pudding, or *hardtack*. Find these and other authentic pioneer recipes in *The Little House Cookbook: Frontier Foods From Laura Ingalls Wilder's Classic Stories* by Barbara M. Walker (Harper & Row, 1979). Ask students to guess what foods might be found in pioneer cupboards, root cellars, springhouses, or smokehouses. Then divide your class into groups and have each group look through the cookbook to discover staples that were common in pioneer kitchens. Aid groups in choosing recipes that can be prepared with the help of parent volunteers.

After sampling some frontier foods, let students quench their thirst with a cupful of homemade *switchel* (ginger water) or lemonade; then review how food preparation has changed since pioneer times. Ask what foods your students would miss if they lived on the frontier. What would they be eating instead of pizza, hamburgers, and French fries?

Welcome To A Quilting Bee

Take the chill out of the cold winter days ahead and bring a part of the American frontier to life by having your students create their own classroom quilt. Read *The Quilt Story* by Tony Johnston, illustrated by Tomie dePaola (G. P. Putnam's Sons, 1985). Discuss the value of a quilt handed down from generation to generation. Not only did quilts provide warmth, they also provided memories of family events. Students will be eager to design their own quilt squares, with each square representing a piece of their own lives. Set up a special display area in your classroom with books on quilts and quilt making. Ask other teachers or local quilt guild members for quilts that you can borrow for your display. Or ask if they would give a class demonstration. Then plan to make a class quilt from cloth or paper squares (see page 92).

Watch Out For The Big Wind

Your students will be "blown away" by a hilarious story written by Carol Purdy and illustrated by Steven Kellogg (Dial Books For Young Readers, 1985). When pioneers settled in the West, they encountered vast, open prairies and threatening weather conditions. After reading *Iva Dunnit And The Big Wind,* your students will learn what happens to one fictitious pioneer family when the wind kicks up!

For a lesson in geography, your students will enjoy adding another chapter that tells where Old Doc Fenton winds up after getting caught in the Big Wind again. Provide a map of the United States and have each student choose a state where his character lands. (Older students may do research to find facts about their states.) Then have each student write and illustrate a story telling what Old Doc found when he landed. Have students share their stories and locate where on the map Old Doc landed. Bind the stories together in a class book called "The Big Wind Dunnit Again."

Tell A Tall Tale

Storytelling was a popular activity for the early settlers. Some stories were humorous and some told about courageous acts. Story-tellers told about the people that the pioneers met or the country that they settled. As the stories were told over and over again, they developed into some real whoppers of tales known as *tall tales.*

For some creative thinking, read some tall tales to your students and have them practice telling their own versions. Some examples include stories about folk heroes such as Paul Bunyan, Pecos Bill, and John Henry. Before creating new adventures, remind students to use exaggerations, descriptive adjectives, and colorful settings or natural wonders such as the Rocky Mountains, Niagara Falls, and the Grand Canyon. Show students where these settings are located on a U.S. map. Have students sit in a circle around a classroom campfire. Ask volunteers to be the storytellers and share their tall tales.

Next have your students write their tall tales on tall sheets of paper. Provide each student with a sheet of lined chart paper. Tell each student to illustrate his tale with large, colorful characters. Then display the stories in the hall for everyone to enjoy.

"Clementine"

In a cavern, in a canyon, excavating for a mine
Dwelt a miner, '49-er, and his daughter,
    Clementine.

O my darling (3x) Clementine!
You are lost and gone forever; dreadful sorry,
    Clementine.

Light she was and like a fairy and her shoes
    were number nine.
Herring boxes without topses, sandals were for
    Clementine.

Drove she ducklings to the water every morn
    ing just at nine;
Stubbed her toe against a splinter, fell into the
    foaming brine.

Ruby lips above the water, blowing bubbles
    soft and fine.
But alas! I was no swimmer, so I lost my
    Clementine.

Strike It Rich!

Gold was discovered in California in 1848. By 1849 thousands of pioneers were on their way to seek their fortunes. These pioneers in search of gold became known as the *forty-niners.* Miners sometimes panned for gold by hand, swirling water and dirt in an ordinary washbowl. Gold would sink to the bottom of the bowl, as dirt and pebbles spilled out. Few miners actually found gold, but your students can "strike it rich" with this activity!

To introduce the gold rush that accelerated westward expansion, teach the ballad of poor "Clementine" below. Ask students if they would want to be forty-niners and have them tell why or why not. Invite a member of a local gem-and-mineral club to bring in samples of minerals miners might encounter in the earth. Have students compare a real gold nugget and *fool's gold* (iron pyrite). Can students tell which is real? Lead students to discover the meaning of the saying, "All that glitters is not gold." Have students examine the real sample, and together list words that describe gold. Ask, "Why do you think gold is so valuable?" Explain that not only is gold rare, but it is also a soft metal that can be easily shaped into coins, jewelry, and art objects.

To complete your science lesson, let your students try panning for gold right in your class-room! Fill a large tub with water and clean play sand. Spray-paint some pebbles gold and hide them in the sand. Demonstrate how to scoop sand in the pan and swirl it in the water to look for the gold nuggets. Pair students and provide each twosome with an aluminum pie pan to pan for gold. Graph the number of gold nuggets found by each child on a large classroom graph. Who will "strike it rich"?

Pack A Prairie Schooner!

1. Draw and color a covered wagon in Wednesday's box.
2. Draw and color a buffalo in Monday's box.
3. Write the name of a famous pioneer or tall-tale hero in Saturday's box.
4. Make Friday's box into a quilt square.
5. Draw an American Indian in Thursday's box.
6. Write the name of a food eaten by the pioneers in Tuesday's box.
7. Draw and color a one-room schoolhouse in Sunday's box.

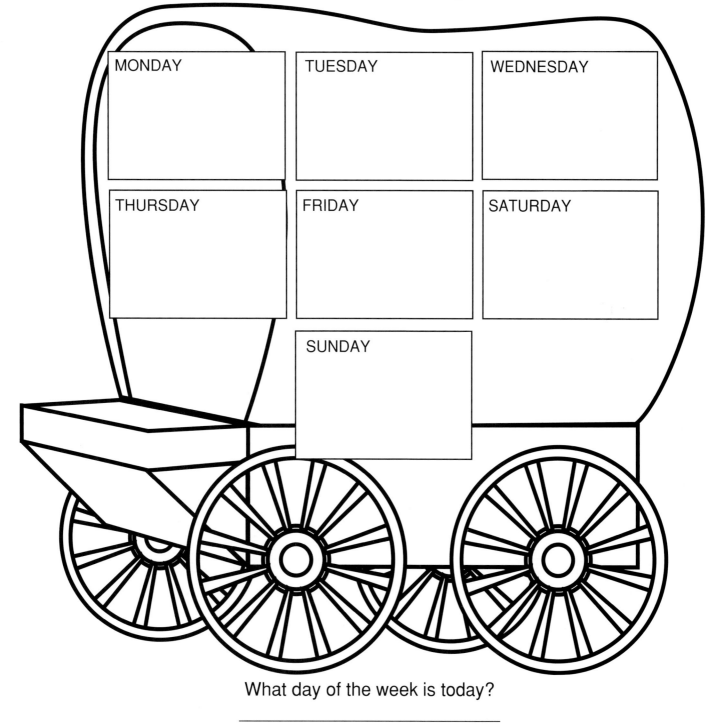

MONDAY   TUESDAY   WEDNESDAY

THURSDAY   FRIDAY   SATURDAY

SUNDAY

What day of the week is today?

_____

ANIMALS IN WINTER

Brrr! It's getting cold outside! Help your youngsters learn about the different strategies that animals use to survive the winter months.

by Stacie Stone

PREPARING FOR WINTER

A student-made booklet will help students understand how animals prepare for winter. To make a booklet, each student will need a copy of the booklet cover and the booklet pages found on pages 89–91. Have each student cut along the heavy solid lines bordering each of his booklet pages. Instruct each student to sequence his booklet cover and pages; then staple each student's booklet together. Read and complete each booklet page together using the corresponding cutouts to assist you.

WHAT DO ANIMALS DO IN WINTER?

Read the book *What Do Animals Do In Winter?* by Melvin and Gilda Berger (Ideals Children's Books, 1995). This book details how animals prepare for winter and what they do to survive the cold. After reading, create a bulletin-board display by using two lengths of yarn to divide a bulletin board into three equal sections. Label one bulletin-board section "Hibernates," label the second section "Migrates," and label the third section "Remains Active." During your study of animals in winter, have wildlife magazines available for students' use. Tell students to cut out pictures of animals that hibernate, migrate, or remain active; then assist each student in stapling his pictures to the correct bulletin-board columns.

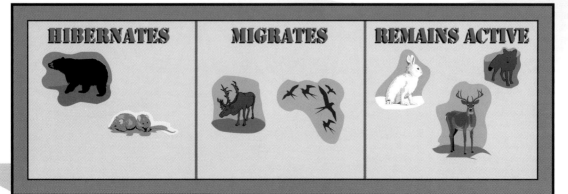

HIBERNATION HAPPENINGS

Some animals survive the long winter months by hibernating, or going into a kind of deep sleep. The animals will awaken when the weather turns warmer and food is more plentiful. To prepare, many hibernating animals eat large quantities of food that is stored as fat, which in turn is used for energy. In an attempt to conserve this energy, a hibernating animal's heartbeat and breathing slow down and its body temperature may drop.

CAVE DWELLERS

Share the story *Every Autumn Comes The Bear* by Jim Arnosky (G. P. Putnam's Sons, 1993) to help students understand that bears find cozy dens (often either a brush pile, a hole in a hillside, or a cave) in which to sleep during the winter months. Then ask students if they would enjoy sleeping most of the winter away. If your students think this might be fun, enlist their help in making a classroom cave in which they can "hibernate."

To make a cave, ask for a donation of a large appliance box. Carefully cut away a portion of the box so that students can enter and exit the cave. Then provide students with sponges and gray and brown tempera paints. Have students sponge-paint the box to resemble a cave. After the paint is dry, allow each student to have a turn hibernating in the cave. As each student awakens from his "sleep" and emerges from the cave, ask him to describe his hibernation experience.

BATTY BATS

Tell students that although some bats migrate in order to find a better food supply or a better place to spend the winter, most North American bats hibernate in caves during the winter months. Then share a bat-related book, such as *A First Look At Bats* by Millicent Selsam and Joyce Hunt (Walker & Co., 1991). Afterward have your students make some construction-paper bats to suspend from the ceiling of your classroom cave. To make a bat, each student will need a brown construction-paper copy of the bat pattern on page 87. Instruct each student to cut out the bat and then fold on the dotted lines as shown. Punch a hole at the bottom of the bat and then tie a length of string through the hole. To suspend the bats, tape the strings to the roof of the cave.

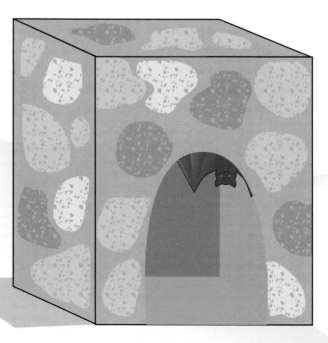

MAGNIFICENT MIGRATION

Migration is the movement of animals to places that offer better living conditions. These improved living conditions often include more favorable weather conditions or more abundant food supplies. Migrations can take place in the air, water, or on land. Seasonal migrations occur twice a year and correlate to changes in temperature and rainfall. During the winter migration some animals travel from north to south in search of warmer weather, while some mountain-dwelling animals migrate from areas of high altitude to areas of lower altitude.

CARIBOU JOURNEY

Barren-ground caribou are animals that make yearly migrations. During the summer months, the caribou spend their days grazing on the Arctic tundra for grasses and leaves. In winter, caribou can be found feeding on lichen in the evergreen forests south of the tundra. Read the book *A Caribou Journey* by Debbie S. Miller (Little, Brown and Company; 1994) to give your students insights into the lives and migrations of caribou.

After reading the book, discuss how the caribou are well-suited for life in their environment. List the caribou's adaptations on a chart like the one shown. Conclude the lesson by dividing students into two groups. Give each group a length of bulletin-board paper, paintbrushes, and various colors of tempera paints. Using the book as a reference, have one group create a mural showing the caribou during the summer months, and have the other group create a mural showing the caribou during the winter months. Display the murals in the hallway for all to see.

HOW THE CARIBOU IS SUITED TO ITS ENVIROMENT	
FEATURE	FUNCTION
hollow fur hair	In winter this insulates the animal from the cold. In summer it helps it float in the water.
hooves	They are insulated with fatty tissue that works like antifreeze. In winter the caribou's broad hooves are used like shovels to find food. In summer the hooves help the animal paddle through the water.
dewclaws	They support the caribou while it's walking through snow.

LONG-DISTANCE TRAVELERS

The arctic tern travels farther than any other migrating bird. Its round-trip travel takes this seabird from the Arctic Circle to the Antarctic Circle and back again. This adds up to a total distance of 22,000 miles! Share this information with your students and then use a map to show them the route that an arctic tern takes when it migrates. Place a series of sticky dots on a large wall map to show students the route that arctic terns follow when they fly from the Arctic Circle to the Antarctic Circle. Then use another set of sticky dots to show the south-north route from the Antarctic Circle back to the Arctic Circle. Conclude the lesson by having students imagine and then discuss what it might be like to take a journey such as this.

ANIMALS THAT STAY ACTIVE

Some animals neither hibernate nor migrate during the winter months. Animals such as foxes, deer, mice, and rabbits remain active during the long winter months. If possible, take your students on a nature walk around your school grounds to look for signs of animals that remain active during the winter; then draw upon these observations while engaging in the following activities.

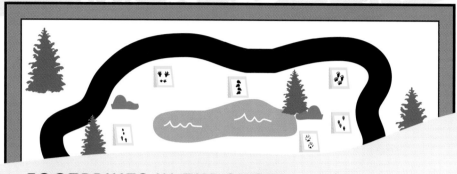

FOOTPRINTS IN THE SNOW

Remind students that some animals remain active throughout the winter months and that they must forage for food. Explain that we might see evidence of their travels when we see their tracks in the snow. Then read a book about animal tracks such as *Footprints In The Snow* by Cynthia Benjamin (Scholastic Inc., 1994) or *Animal Tracks* by Arthur Dorros (Scholastic Inc., 1991).

Afterward enlist students' help in creating a bulletin board that helps them learn to identify different animals' tracks. Begin by covering a bulletin board with white construction paper. Use a black permanent marker to draw a path on the bulletin board as shown. Have students cut trees, bushes, and ponds from construction paper; then staple the cutouts to the board. Next fold each of six 4" x 9" construction-paper strips in half. Mount an animal-track picture to each of the six top flaps and the corresponding animal picture to each of the bottom flaps. (See the patterns on page 88.) Staple the resulting cards to various locations on the bulletin board. Students try to identify what animals made the tracks, then lift the card flaps to reveal the correct answers.

KEEP LOOKING!

The book *Keep Looking!* by Millicent Selsam and Joyce Hunt (Macmillan Publishing Company, 1989) is a must for any unit on animals in winter. This book's beautiful illustrations and wealth of information add up to a perfect teaching combination. After reading this book to your youngsters, discuss how the use of bird feeders attracted animals to the home featured in the story. Then show students a small bird feeder and tell them that you will hang it outside the window. Explain to students that it will be their job to keep track of animals that come to the bird feeder.

Next show your students a classroom area that has been stocked with juvenile field guides about birds, mammals, and tracks; a pair of inexpensive binoculars; sheets of notebook paper; pencils; and crayons. You may even wish to place an inexpensive instant camera at the center so that students can catch some animals in action. Encourage students to use these items during scheduled observation periods to write observations and sketch birds or other animals that were witnessed. Plan to walk outside every few days to look for tracks of animals who have been searching for tasty treats that have fallen out of the feeder.

ANIMALS IN WINTER: A PLAY

Perform this play for parents as a culminating event for your animals-in-winter unit. Have some children play the part of trees and other forest animals so that each child has a part in the play. For costumes have each student glue a picture of his animal to a construction-paper sign that he can wear around his neck. For scenery, use the student-made cave as the focal point, and place a blue sheet or table cloth on the floor to serve as a pond. If desired, have groups of students paint murals to hang as part of the scenery. While students are performing, have an adult videotape the play so that students can have an opportunity to see the performance.

Characters:

Narrator One	Wally Woodchuck	Sally Snowshoe Rabbit	Gary Goose
Donna Dormouse	Freddy Fox	Rhonda Rabbit	Barry Bear
Narrator Two	Franny Fox	Tim Turtle	Sammy Snake
David Deer	Wendy Woodchuck	Betsy Beaver	

The Setting: In a forest where all of the animals except Gary Goose are going about their daily routines. *(Have students stand in groups according to whether they hibernate or stay active during winter months.)*
The Time: November

Narrator One: Welcome to our play about animals in winter. We hope this play will help you understand how different animals prepare for winter.

Gary Goose: *(enters carrying a suitcase)* Hi, everyone! It's that time of year again. I'm getting ready to migrate.

Rhonda Rabbit: Mi-what?!

Gary Goose: Migrate! I fly for hundreds of miles in order to reach my final destination—a warmer area far south of here.

Franny Fox: Why are you leaving? Why don't you stay here and hunt for mice and rabbits like I do?

Gary Goose: I don't think that would be such a good idea for me.

Franny Fox: Why not?

Gary Goose: It would be hard for me to catch and eat mice and rabbits like you do. And you grow extra fur to help you stay warm during the cold winter. I'm afraid I wouldn't be able to stay warm and find food if I stayed here. Besides, I'll have a nice warm place to stay once I reach the south.

Sammy Snake: Well, where will you stay?

Gary Goose: Years ago my uncle Gabe showed me a nice pond near a golf course. I've been going there every year since.

Wendy Woodchuck: It sure must be hard to fly all that way. Why don't you stay here and hibernate with me and some of my other friends?

Gary Goose: Hibernate? What does that mean?

Wally Woodchuck: When animals hibernate that means that they sleep most of the winter away in their wintertime homes.

Gary Goose: Don't you get hungry?

86

Donna Dormouse: No, not really. I've been busy this fall searching for food and eating, and eating, and eating.

Gary Goose: I think I get it—you eat lots of food so that you get fat. Then your body uses the fat while you're fast asleep, right?

Donna Dormouse: Exactly!

Barry Bear: But some hibernating animals like me wake up during the winter and nibble on food. Sometimes in the middle of winter I'll wake up and wish I had a big bowl of berries to eat.

Tim Turtle: Other hibernating animals–like me and my friends Mr. Frog, Mr. Toad, Miss Lizard, Mrs. Snake, and Miss Turtle–sleep the whole winter through. When the cold weather comes, we hibernate. We don't wake up until the weather turns warm again and our body temperatures rise.

Gary Goose: I guess it's pretty quiet around here in winter with so many animals gone and the rest are sleeping.

David Deer: Oh, not all of us hibernate or migrate. Some animals, like me, stay active during the winter months.

Betsy Beaver: I hide in my lodge during the winter. All summer long my busy-beaver friends and I cut down trees with our teeth. We store the wood pieces inside our dry, warm lodges and then in winter we munch on the bark. Mmm, tasty!

Sally Snowshoe Rabbit: I go out hunting for food in winter. And I get a new coat each winter because my fur changes from brown to white. My enemies have a harder time seeing me in the snow. *(looks nervously at fox who is standing next to her)*

Freddy Fox: Don't worry, Sally. I won't eat you.

Gary Goose: *(looking up at sky)* Well, it looks like snow. I'm going to meet the rest of my flock; then we'll head south. See you all in the spring! Have a terrific winter! *(exits stage waving)*

All: Bye, Gary! Fly safely!

Narrator Two: *(to audience)* Thank you for coming to our play.

Bat Pattern

Use with "Batty Bats" on page 83.

Animal Tracks Patterns

Use with "Footprints In The Snow" on page 85.

Rabbit

Bear

Deer

Beaver

Fox

Mouse

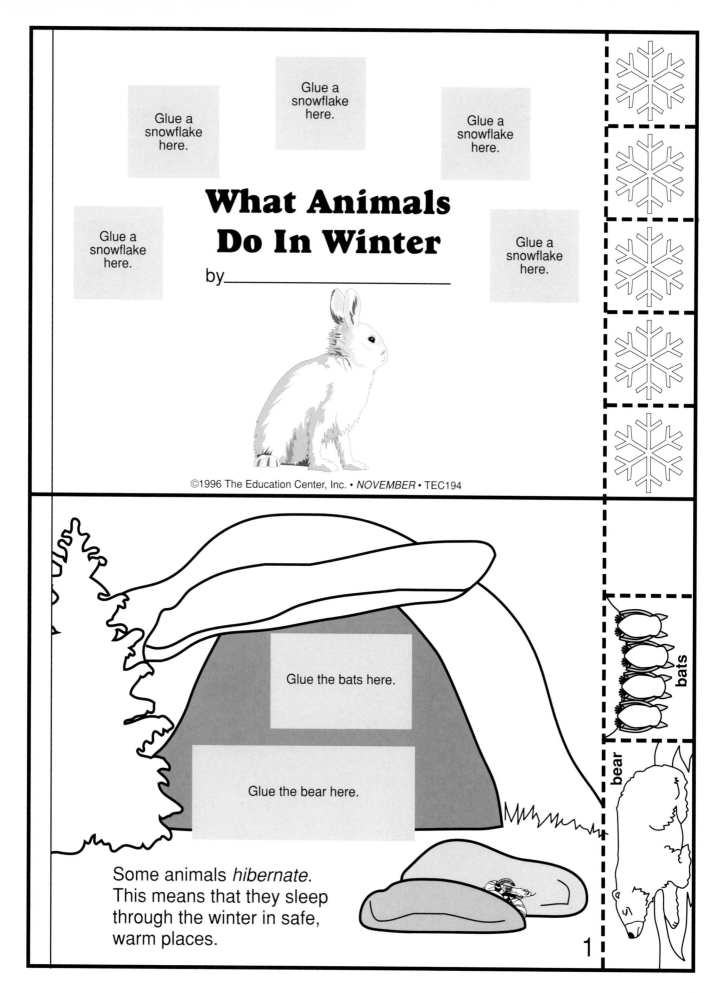

Glue a snowflake here.

Glue a snowflake here.

Glue a snowflake here.

Glue a snowflake here.

Glue a snowflake here.

What Animals Do In Winter

by_____

©1996 The Education Center, Inc. • *NOVEMBER* • TEC194

Glue the bats here.

Glue the bear here.

bats

bear

Some animals *hibernate.* This means that they sleep through the winter in safe, warm places.

1

89

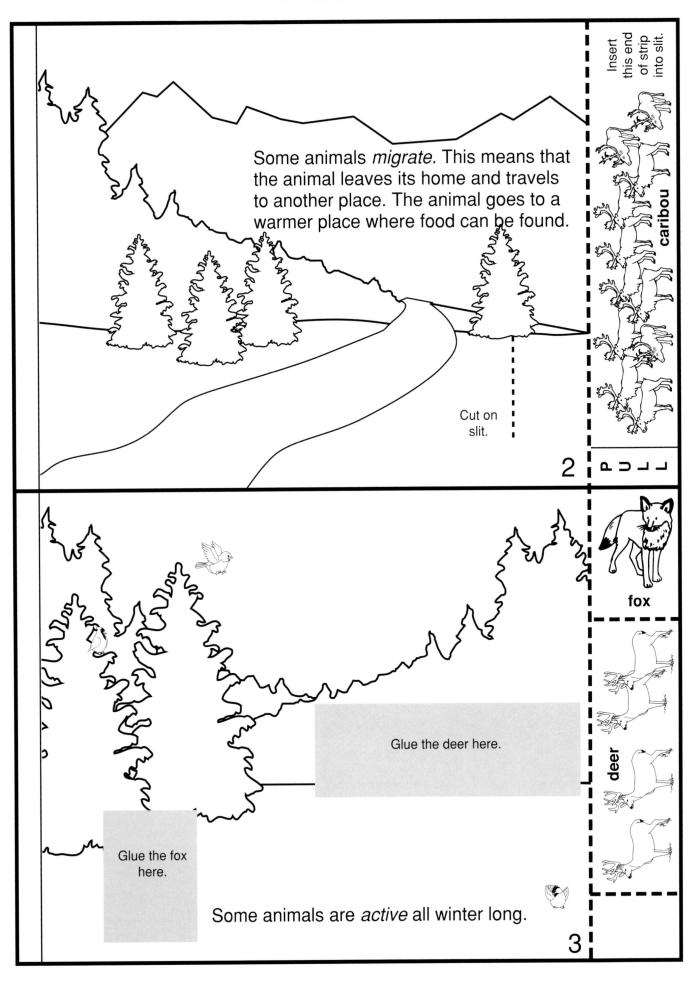

caribou

Some animals *migrate.* This means that the animal leaves its home and travels to another place. The animal goes to a warmer place where food can be found.

Cut on slit.

2

P U L L

fox

deer

Glue the deer here.

Glue the fox here.

Some animals are *active* all winter long.

3

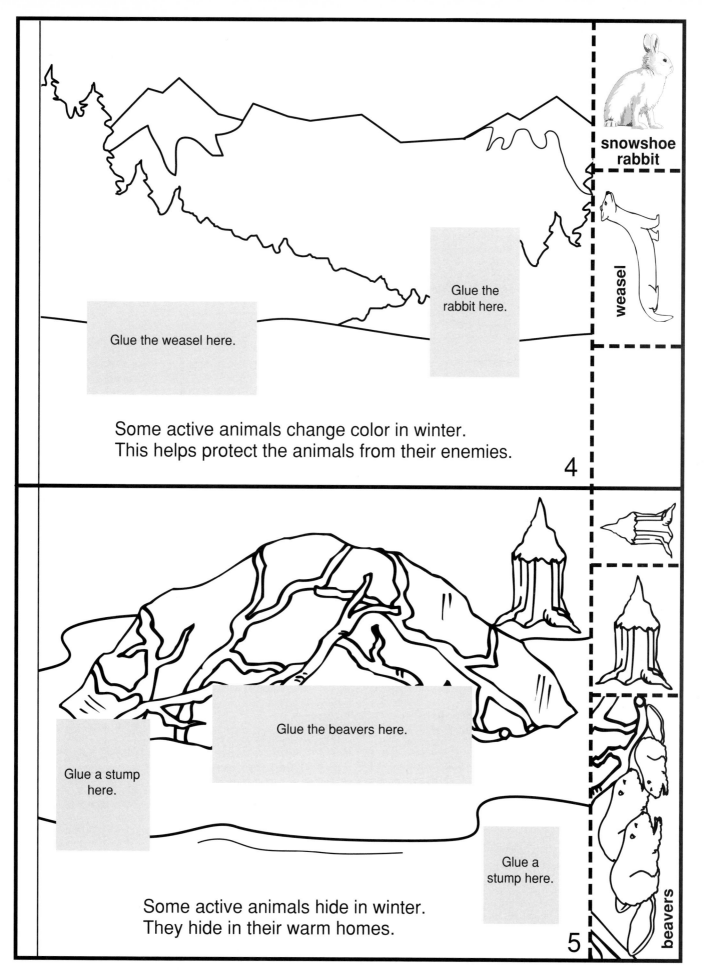

snowshoe rabbit

weasel

Glue the rabbit here.

Glue the weasel here.

Some active animals change color in winter.
This helps protect the animals from their enemies.

4

beavers

Glue the beavers here.

Glue a stump here.

Glue a stump here.

Some active animals hide in winter.
They hide in their warm homes.

5

Quilts
Patchwork From Past To Present

The technique for making quilted cloth dates back to the Egyptians and was introduced into Europe at the end of the eleventh century by the crusaders returning from the Holy Wars. The colorful designs and brilliant patterns of quilts are just as popular today. These activities are sure to get your students interested in the fascinating world of quilting!

Ideas by Sherri Beckwith and Kathy Wolf

From Rags To Keepsakes

In the early days of quilting, women created quilts from scraps of worn-out clothes, old curtains, and beloved blankets. The quilters sorted the scraps and arranged them to create patterns that were pleasing to the eye. Each piece was a reminder of the past as well. Your youngsters can discover new and exciting designs in much the same way!

At a quilting center, provide a box of wallpaper samples, leftover gift wrap, and construction-paper scraps along with a basket filled with pieces of fabric, ribbon, and lace. (Ask parents to clean out their rag bags and allow children to bring in pieces to add to the scrap box.) Provide a supply of 8" x 8" cardboard squares. Have students work in pairs to mix and match materials to create color-coordinated quilt squares. Have each student cut and glue her pieces to cover her cardboard square. Challenge students to piece their squares together by placing them side by side on a flat surface to make a larger design.

Could It Be A Quilting Bee?

Since the early nineteenth century, women have gathered around tables for quilting and conversation. The Amish still carry on this tradition today. In addition to serving as a social time, quilting bees are a form of mutual aid and preserve a sense of community among the Amish people.

Encourage this sense of community in your own classroom by hosting a quilting bee of your own! Provide each student with an eight-inch square of muslin and ask her to draw a picture or symbols to represent an important event in her life. Students can use permanent fabric markers or crayons for their designs. Sew the squares together by machine or give the squares to an experienced quilter to complete.

For a simpler version, provide eight-inch paper squares on which students can draw their designs. Arrange and glue the paper squares on a large piece of butcher paper. Gather a piece of crepe paper and glue it around the edge of the paper quilt for a fancy border. Display the completed quilt in your library or school lobby.

Name That Quilt!

The history of quilt patterns is as intriguing as the quilts themselves. Some patterns were designed and named to commemorate events in our country's history, such as "Underground Railroad" or "Sherman's March." Others were named to honor individuals, such as the patterns called "Martha Washington's Star" and "Lincoln's Platform." Share *The Quilt-Block History Of Pioneer Days With Projects Kids Can Make* by Mary Cobb (The Millbrook Press, 1995). Then engage students in a fun quilt-naming activity that results in booklets of their own personal patterns.

Display several popular patterns, such as the "Double Wedding Ring" or the "Dresden Plate," that you have located in a quilt book. (Most contain beautifully colored pictures.) Give each student five index cards; five pint-sized, zippered plastic storage bags; and five seven-inch squares cut from colored construction paper. Have the child cut his index cards to create four-inch squares and save the excess. On the blank side of each of four squares, instruct the student to create an original quilt pattern. On the lined side of the leftover piece of card, each student should name his pattern and write a brief history or explanation of the name. For instance, one child might name his pattern "Mother's Flowers" because it reminds him of roses which his mom grows. Instruct the student to use his fifth card to design a cover for his booklet. Demonstrate how to mount each design on a construction-paper square, glue its description to the back, and insert the square into an individual plastic bag. Zip up the bags. Have each student arrange his bags in the correct order and staple twice along the zippered side as shown to create a Quilt Pattern Booklet. Display these in your reading center for all to enjoy!

Quilting For Math

Give a bucket of pattern blocks to a small group of students and let them invent beautiful patterns that would be the envy of even the most seasoned quilters. At your math center, provide pattern blocks and quilt patterns for students to replicate.

Or set up a symmetry center with 9" x 9" laminated cards illustrated with half of a symmetrical quilt design (see the sample at right). Provide Vis-à-Vis® markers for the student to complete the design on the blank side. Students will soon learn the meaning of symmetry and look for it in quilts!

The Album Quilt

An album quilt was a special kind of quilt made as a remembrance for a family or friend moving west. Each block was completed by a different neighbor or friend and signed by the quilter. The blocks were assembled, quilted, and presented at a going-away party. Album quilts were treasured reminders of those left behind and were displayed in places of honor.

To make an album for a classmate or teacher who is moving, provide each child with a precut paper square. Have each child color a picture on the square, add stitching, and sign his name. Mount each square on black construction paper and punch a hole in the top as shown. Line up the pages, punch holes, and assemble with metal rings to make a keepsake album for the person who is leaving.

Patchwork Poetry

A *patchwork* is a covering made of pieces of cloth of various colors and shapes that have been sewn together. Create this patchwork bulletin board to display original poetry.

First, create a class poem to model the process. Choose a starter word such as a student's name or a season. Ask volunteers to offer descriptive words that begin with each letter of the word and describe the word. For example:

> **S**unny
> **U**nbearable
> **M**ostly hot
> **M**akes me thirsty
> **E**xciting outdoors
> **R**estful

Then have students write their own patchwork poetry. Mount each poem on a different-colored construction-paper shape. Arrange the patches on a bulletin board with the title "A Patchwork Of Poems."

Quilting ABCs

Create a one-of-a-kind quilt to hang in the classroom throughout the school year. Assign a letter of the alphabet to each student. Provide paper of various colors from which children can cut out their letters. Have each child glue his letter to a solid-color paper square. Scrap pieces can be used to cut out things that begin with that letter. For instance, a square with the letter *A* on it could also have an apple, an ant, and an ax glued around it. These squares can be assembled and glued to a large piece of butcher paper to create a classroom quilt that your students will surely want to show off!

More Books About Quilting

The Boy And The Quilt by Shirley Kurtz (Good Books®, 1991)

The Boy And The Cloth Of Dreams by Jenny Koralek (Candlewick Press, 1994)

The Josephina Story Quilt by Eleanor Coerr (HarperCollins Publishers, 1986)

A Patchwork Of Books

Discover how quilts have journeyed across oceans and cultures, providing generations with links to the past. This endearing selection of quilting stories will capture the hearts of your students and stimulate conversations about families and traditions.

The Quilt Story
by Tony Johnston
(G. P. Putnam's Sons, 1985)

This book will appeal to any child who has sought comfort in a familiar blanket or stuffed animal. Painted in grand folk-art tradition, the illustrations will take the listeners' imaginations back to the past on the prairie.

After reading, discuss how the young girl found comfort in an old quilt when she had to move to a new home. Ask how the quilt warmed the hearts of two generations. Explain that quilts are often labors of love passed down by families and treasured as reminders of family events. Introduce the word *keepsake.* Ask children to tell about keepsakes they are saving, or to think of items they can hand down to their children.

The Patchwork Quilt
by Valerie Flournoy
(Dial Books For Young Readers, 1985)

Tanya and her grandmother share special moments together making a glorious quilt. Each piece is unique in that it carries a fond memory. When Tanya's grandmother becomes ill, Tanya searches for a way to help her.

After reading the story, discuss how we can give of ourselves to brighten the day of someone in need. Then provide materials for students to make patchwork greetings for residents of a local nursing home. Have each child color a paper square and add a greeting as shown. Mount the squares on a large piece of bulletin-board paper to make a quilt. Displayed on a wall, it's sure to brighten someone's day!

The Mountains Of Quilt
by Nancy Willard
(Harcourt Brace Jovanovich Publishers, 1987)

Enter the world of magic as four magicians entertain your students. Amidst all the hocus-pocus, the magicians discover their magic carpet is missing. The grandmother who finds the carpet thinks it's just what she needs to complete her quilt. The adventure continues as the mighty magicians try to reclaim their carpet square.

For creative writing, have each student write and illustrate a story about a magic quilt. Ask students, "What magic powers does your quilt have? Where can it take you?" Have students share their stories and illustrations. Place the stories for all to read in a treasure chest at your reading center. If you wish, provide a magic quilt or carpet for students to sit on as they read. Reading takes you to magical places!

The Keeping Quilt
by Patricia Polacco
(Simon and Schuster Children's Books, 1988)

This heartwarming story spans a century and crosses the ocean from Russia. Your students will be intrigued as a quilt is transformed from a Sabbath tablecloth, to a wedding canopy, to a blanket that welcomes new babies!

Follow up with this activity that encourages self-esteem and respect for the uniqueness of each individual. Ask each student to bring in a snippet of material from a favorite old blanket or a garment he once wore. Or he may bring in a piece of clothing of which he is particularly proud, such as a sports uniform or ball cap. Give each student a large piece of drawing paper and ask him to re-create the *pattern* of the fabric. Have each student share his illustration, describe the fabric, and tell what memories the pattern brings to mind. For example, a student may say her teddy bears and hearts were on a favorite pair of pajamas Grandma gave her for Christmas when she was six. You may want to share your own special fabric and special memories from an old prom dress or favorite tie!

Luka's Quilt
by Georgia Guback
(Greenwillow Books, 1994)

Explore Hawaiian traditions with Luka and her grandmother, Tutu. Their close relationship is one that will inspire talks about the bond between generations as well as loving and forgiving those we love. Tutu makes a quilt as a gift for Luka, but it is not what the girl expects. Their relationship is strained, but the festivities of a special Hawaiian holiday bring them back together.

After your discussion, explore the fantastic colors and patterns of Hawaii with this art project. Display some Hawaiian-print fabrics and have students use tracing paper to copy and color the designs. Mount the tracing-paper samples on squares of colored construction paper. Display them on a wall or bind them into a class book.

The Patchwork Farmer
by Craig Brown
(Greenwillow Books, 1989)

Follow the farmer in this wordless picture book as he works in his fields, tearing his overalls a little each day. Luckily he has a big basket of patches. As summer progresses, the basket empties and the farmer's overalls begin to look like a patchwork quilt!

Create some patchwork overalls for this eye-catching classroom display. Use pinking shears to cut a supply of paper squares. Provide each student with a 9" x 12" piece of dark blue construction paper plus a three-inch square for a pocket. Demonstrate how to cut a *V* shape as shown to create a pair of pants. Have each student glue his pocket and construction-paper patches to his cutout. Then have him add stitching with a marker and tuck a handkerchief in the pocket. Use clothespins to clip the patched overalls to a clothesline stretched across your class-room. What a colorful wash day!